They All Ran After
the Farmer's Wife

They All Ran After the Farmer's Wife

VERONICA FRATER

Farming Press

First published 1990

Copyright © Veronica Frater, 1990

British Library Cataloguing in Publication Data

Frater, Veronica
They all ran after the farmer's wife.
1. England. Agriculture
I. Title
630.942

ISBN 0-85236-214-5

Published by Farming Press Books
4 Friars Courtyard, 30–32 Princes Street
Ipswich IP1 1RJ, United Kingdom

Distributed in North America
by Diamond Farm Enterprises,
Box 537, Alexandria Bay, NY 13607, USA

Title and Half-title cartoons by Andrew Frater

Typeset by Galleon Photosetting, Ipswich
Printed and bound in Great Britain by
Mackays of Chatham PLC, Chatham, Kent

They All Ran After
the Farmer's Wife

January

'Blocked in? No, we never get blocked in down here. No, never. Coastal plain, you know.' The faces of the summer bed and breakfast guests register this information, their minds doubtless casting back to the classroom, the geography of their schooldays. What was it now? 'The sea warms the land. . . .'

. . . So here we are, at the beginning of a New Year, full of resolutions and party fare – blocked in. Yes, it has happened. In the last fifteen years in this bleak and windswept spot, we have been cut off before just once; it did not last and it did not have the ferocity of this meteorological horror.

It started snowing yesterday and did not stop. Little notice was taken at first, but slowly the landscape disappeared under huge white mounds called drifts. I suppose it is a blizzard really, the snow combined with the familiar strong winds. The children have been sent home from school, much to their delight. When the bus deposits them, the driver shakes his head grimly and announces with drama to the world in general that he knows not when he will be back. The kids are over the moon; they love it. They have been outside more today than days in July. Snowmen have been fashioned in quantity – let's face it, we rarely receive sufficient material any winter for even a small gnome. Snowball battles have been won and lost; someone has ambitiously begun an igloo. They come in with sparkling eyes and rosy cheeks. It is an ill wind. . . .

It's an ill wind all right. The TV Weatherman stands there in his natty suit, handkerchief matching his tie, in his nice, centrally heated studio, smiling the news that this lot has come straight from Siberia; this is why we on the east coast are copping it for a change. Living miles off the beaten track (A1), half-buried in the sand on the north-eastern corner of England, we will feel it more than most. Still smiling, he goes on to declare that there is more to come and, according to his charts, no sign of change. This is bad news. I only hope that we have enough Weetabix, whisky and disposable nappies to last the duration.

I wake in what feels like 'the wee small hours', open my eyes and see absolutely nothing. Now, in a house full of children, where all-night illumination abounds, this can only mean one thing – a power cut. Oh no! It is no use throwing myself on the floor, screaming, begging to be taken away, as no one could get through to take me away. Must be sensible about it. I struggle out of bed and grope my way downstairs, cursing the odd Lego piece my tender foot finds – or worse, one of those plastic horned cows of which the little people are so fond.

At last, I find my way to the dairy and grope for the candle box. Soon, I have one upright beacon on my saucer and, armed with more and a box of matches, feeling like Wee Willie Winkie, I stumble round the house, erecting lights in strategic spots. The next job is to telephone the Board, who receive the news without enthusiasm.

It is now 2.35 am, I discover by the mechanical clock in the kitchen, and I crawl wearily back to bed where guess who is blissfully unaware of this new development. After a brief moment of hesitation, a decision is reached that he should be informed, the instrument chosen being the horned head of a plastic cow. He regains consciousness, protestingly, and at my words, groans, 'Christ' and promptly starts to snore again.

It is so quiet. No buzzing of the boiler, no World Service which usually drones out all night from the mains radio, no noise outside either as all is muffled by the thick blanket of snow. At last I drift (ha) off and am awakened at a slightly more civilised hour by a baby's crying beside my bed. She doesn't seem to mind these straitened circumstances, as long as her simple physical demands are dealt with. Then, the house slowly starts to come to life as heads appear one by one.

'What's happened?'

'Why is it dark?'

'Why isn't the telly working?'

I should explain that even if it is becoming lighter outside, the house remains in darkness. This is because our Siberian friend has plastered snow all over our windows and there it has remained, forming freezing curtains outside; this cannot be regarded as total catastrophy as we have few curtains inside and, at least, the crystals have blocked up some of the cracks which usually admit draught.

Everyone is instructed to go back to bed and stay there until further notice. This is great fun apparently. It won't last; they will soon feel the pangs of hunger and mass movement below will be necessary. I wonder how long a candle lasts. Power failures we have suffered before, dozens, but never ones we couldn't drive away from – for lunch in a bright warm café or to camp out temporarily at Granny's house, she hoping for a return to normal services more fervently than us.

Where are those lamps I purchased from the thermal underwear catalogue for just such a contingency as this? Here they are, but of course, I never got round to buying the correct battery. In this house, batteries abound. We have batteries for cassette recorders, batteries for cars, batteries for games, walkie-talkie sets . . . but not, it would seem, batteries to fit these useful emergency lamps. This farmer's wife wears a great deal of thermal underwear, incidentally – even in a normal winter of only icy gales and floods. Then, there is another thing – the central heating system (by which I mean that old monstrosity of a boiler in the back kitchen, which heats the water and by way of the odd antiquated radiator, takes the chill off parts of this rambling old house human beings rarely reach) is off as, even though it is oil-fired, it is ignited by electric power.

The telephone rings.

'Happy Birthday, dear!'

It is my mother. I am not pleased about birthdays at the best of times and this clearly is not one of them. I bite back one or two rude exclamations and receive her salutations as graciously as possible. It seems that her village is blocked in too but then, there is shop, pub, neighbours. She sympathises with our plight and I go into the kitchen where everyone is now huddled round our old friend, the Aga, which is also old and uneconomical but so comforting. We wonder what to do next. Breakfast would seem naturally to be the next item on the agenda.

Having a large family means many things. Being able to mop up all the cereal offers going at any one time is one of them. The centre of our large kitchen table looks like a model of New York's skyline, with tall packets waiting to be emptied. It is a rare phenomenon for two family members to eat the same variety, although the straw-like bales are acceptable to most. Packets are finished at an alarming rate and shopping is a nightmare, there being little room in the trolley for more sophisticated items like yogurt (purchased in 12s) or tins of baked beans. If there is booty secreted inside the packet, the inner bag is deftly removed and examined, with up to six pairs of hands palpating the contents. If the sought-after prize is spotted near the bottom of the packet, there are showers of cereal everywhere, as arms disappear up to the elbow for its entry into the world . . . and subsequent serving is difficult.

The meal is lingered over today – a strange state of affairs, in contrast to the usual pre-school bus panic and cries of 'where's my packed lunch/homework/trainers/games kit?' and urgency, bordering on bad temper over the passing of the packets, the milk, the sugar, etc. On a normal day after the school bus has been, a great deal of clearing up has to be contended with, not to mention dealing with the needs of what today are termed 'pre-school children'. It is at this point that the farmer usually makes good *his* escape, having left his descent for breakfast until the last possible moment. There are no hard-and-fast rules about the time of his exit, especially in wintertime, as we are worker-less from the end of October until the beginning of March.

Today, however, he seems quite reluctant to go outside at all. That's funny, he always maintains he likes bad weather. Gales he glories in, rain he revels in, etc. Yes, off he goes every day in that dreadful holey old jumper, what could euphemistically be called a body warmer and the threadbare old jacket. Over all goes a heavy-duty plastic coat in a none-too-gentle shade of yellow, looking like a canary with dropsy, the battered old peaked cap completing the picture. However, today, what is this? He is wearing the yellow trousers that go with the coat, and out he goes.

It is not long before he is back again. All the troughs are frozen, so the youngsters in the shed are thirsty; boiling water is necessary here. The fifty or so pedigree ewes have started lambing so they are in the ante- or postnatal wards, and they will naturally require plenty of liquids.

All this takes time before he finally mounts his trusty steed, the tractor, to inspect those further afield. He probably wishes it was a horse this morning because he soon discovers that the diesel has frozen. By the time he has attended to this – so is he. Once the vehicle is operational, he feels quite pleased with himself, sitting up there in his warm cab, listening to the radio, looking down on the wild, white world from a position of superiority. He is out for a considerable period, visiting all the outside stock and Jack's house up the road, from where a 'Mayday' call for fags has been received.

By what used laughingly to be called 'lunchtime' he seems quite sorry to swap his cosy perch for the rather chilly, dimly lit, quiet kitchen – quiet that is except for the odd squeaks and wails. It has been a funny morning for, in addition to being deprived of heat and light, one cannot operate the washing machine, hoover or food processor . . . every cloud has a silver lining.

There is certainly no need to worry about items in the

freezer defrosting or those in the fridge decomposing, as the air temperature surrounding these tools is surely infinitely lower than the standards laid down by the EC for food storage. However, a carton of wholesome soup has been fished from the murky depths – even if the transformation into an appetising snack has its problems. Of course, the usual aid for such a process, the much-maligned or revered microwave (depending upon which side you stand), is non-operational. Therefore, after chiselling it out of the extra large poly-unsaturated margarine tub the resulting cuboid block is being forced unyielding into a round saucepan. Oh dear, even the Aga seems to be cooling now, no doubt due to its continuous use over a long period combined with the wind from Siberia which is wailing through what the children call 'the cow' on the roof.

The phone rings again. At least that instrument is still working, thank goodness, so one does not feel totally divorced from the outside world. It is a friend in town, having heard of our plight, asking if there is anything we want. Well, you know that helicopter you have in your garage. . . . No, I am just hysterical . . . keep in touch.

After a lukewarm lunch, he announces it has stopped snowing.

'Why don't you go out for a walk to cheer yourself up? After all, it is *your birthday*.'

After a moment's thought, it is decided that such a course might be the lesser evil. It is proposed to walk to the golf clubhouse for Jack's cigarettes. What a strange world awaits. The path between farmhouse and farm buildings has gone – disappeared – replaced by a high wall of snow to be negotiated. Once past the farm, progress is a little easier and the road across the golf course is almost visible in parts, such was the fickle nature of the blizzard. The clubhouse is approximately one mile from the house.

There are no golfers either on the course or in the bar. To my astonishment, 'Come in!' cry the Steward and his wife, whom I hardly know. Once my eyes have become accustomed to the gloom of the inner sanctum after the glare of the snow, I recognise the craggy features of the farmer from the next farm, who appears to be sipping from a glass of amber liquid. A glass of something similar is thrust into my own hand – and they don't even know it is my birthday. Within a very short time, I find myself imparting this fact to those present, and life in general feels much more bearable. On my way home I reflect – was this like the wartime camaraderie of which my mother often speaks with such nostalgia and affection? Unlike hill farmers, we see our neighbours rarely. We are all self-contained, wrapped up in our own small worlds. Hooray. As I approach the house, I see an illuminated kitchen! How wonderful!

'Ah, we liked the candles!' cry the children as the waxen stubs are collected up and replaced in the box, ready for the next emergency – God forbid! Perhaps I had better put them on my shopping list (if I ever manage to reach a shop again) – oh, and those batteries! Talking of shopping lists, we appear to be running low on Weetabix. Now this *is* serious; there are some commodities this family simply cannot manage without. Also, the milkman, who only comes three times a week anyway, could not get any farther than the farm on the hill, two miles up the road. This is where wartime philosophy is employed. A couple of telephone calls and an elaborate plan is conceived whereby the tractor from the farm beyond the golf club goes up to the next farm to collect the milk, calling at another house, in which dwells a known Weetabix addict, to pick up a pack on the way. The tractor then carries its valuable cargo back as far as the golf club, from where it is later collected by the grateful head of this household on his tractor. Phew! We can last another day.

I am glad we have no bed and breakfast guests at the moment as stores start to diminish fast all round. One by one, items are withdrawn from the menu. Of course, many farmers' wives will scoff at this point: 'Silly bitch – fancy running out of stores! Fancy not stocking up properly! This happens to us every winter!' This is the point; it simply does not happen to us. Ah well, fresh fruit and vegetables went days ago and now the cupboard is becoming bare. Bread is unbuttered (or polyunsaturated fatted) and then, there is no bread. Beans on cream cracker is just not the same. No more bacon, sausages, cheese . . . the hens stop laying. Oh, surely this cannot last much longer. The TV Weatherman still smiles.

There is a small theatre company staying in the holiday cottage. They came for a fortnight this winter to discuss the coming year's programme. I should imagine that they have their entire repertoire word-perfect by now as there is little else that they can do. They brought all their provisions with them, the 'isolated cottage on the Northumbrian coast' must have sounded like Siberia itself to them, inhabitants of a Midland industrial town. Their only problem seems to be *coal* they inform the man on the tractor; they burn a hundred-weight in twenty-four hours. The coalman would love them. We live in the kitchen, no longer daring to light a fire in our sitting room.

During this bleak period, we do go out for a meal. 'You must be joking', I hear you shriek! No, our neighbour at the house at the far end of the road (just before it peters out), Jack, is away a great deal; his fingers are in various pies. However, when he is here we certainly know about it. Jack is a character – a big man with a big voice and a big personality. We are very fond of Jack although a little goes a long way.

Jack has done many things. You name it, Jack's done it: run a dairy farm, run an exotic fish business in Billingsgate, run a salmon fishery here, owned and learned to fly an aeroplane.

He no longer runs his place as a fishery but outbuildings have been converted to cottages, a swimming pool has been sunk, the conservatory has been transformed into the bar, the garden has been cleared to make a campsite. In short it is now a sort of mini leisure centre.

However, in winter they shut up shop and one morning Jack telephones with the invitation: 'Come to lunch.' Up we all trudge slowly through the snow, and as we approach the White House, Jack rushes out past us without a word. What can he be doing? Ah – all is revealed as he digs a bottle of champagne from a snowdrift, the first of many. I am afraid I cannot describe the lunch, or in fact the rest of the day. The following day, I seem to have a particularly unpleasant virus, affecting stomach and head; husband has something similar. The children seem all right, though.

At last, a change in the weather is sniffed and very slowly life returns to normality. The loos no longer require thawing each morning – a time-consuming operation but so necessary with so many small boys in the house. The troughs outside take a little longer. The drifts gradually disappear and the children go back to school with reluctance.

Not long after their return to school again, they are struck down with a virus one by one. 'There is a lot of it about' at this time of year – everything from a runny nose to pneumonia going under the common heading of 'the flu'. The French have a better word for it (they usually do) and very soon the whole of the neighbourhood is 'gripped' by the bug. The boys' teacher, given to original expression, talks of the class 'going down like flies'.

Having a large family – of diverse personality and constitution – gives one a unique opportunity to study a virus. I bet I could write a paper on the subject, and I might if I were not so downright exhausted after being up night after night tending patients. Of course, the crunch finally comes when his lordship gets it! What was 'a little thing', 'nothing to worry about' over which his wife flapped unnecessarily, becomes much more serious.

What is serious is the fact that he cannot raise himself from his bed to tend his stock. I manage to pin down our temporarily redundant farmworker, Kevin, who is fortunately not winkle-picking at the moment; he does the inside feeding and bedding. Later, when a reasonable level of consciousness is elicited upstairs so that an eye can be kept on the

13

convalescent patients, the farmer's wife dons her wellies and proceeds on the six-mile stroll round the stock.

I like walking round the fields, I really do. I so rarely get the opportunity these days. It is unfortunate that I feel it only fair to strap my youngest infant to my chest to accompany my exercise and that she has not settled down to sleep as she usually does in this position. Her kicking and intermittent wailing tend to diminish the soothing effect of 'being at one with nature'. I take one of the dogs with me, more out of sympathy than anything – being shut up all day cannot be much fun. He looks up at me in surprise, as if thinking 'this is a turn up for the books!'

It is a pity I cannot remember which command he follows, I reflect, as we enter the first field of sheep. Try Scottish; try Northumbrian. I cannot whistle. The dog looks up at me, jaw open, ears half-cocked. I'll swear he is laughing. Oh well, the sheep look all right, as they bunch together, as far away from me as possible in a forty-acre field of the uneven surface of old rig and furrow.

The cows all look all right too. Now, how many are there supposed to be? Was it twenty-three or thirty-two? One, two, three – oh, why do they keep moving? I am sure I have counted that black one twice at least. After four counts with no duplicate totals, I make one final attempt – twenty-six! I don't think I'll mention it unless he asks.

Now for the Blackies, my favourites – or Scottish Black-faces, to call them correctly. These are the characters in the world of sheep – the free-thinkers – spread across the salt grasses, still covered with a sprinkling of snow. How many of these were there supposed to be? I have no intention of counting sheep but the figure one hundred and fifty springs to mind, and as things are at the moment, I can only see three (and extremely lame they are too). Up and down the tussocks I go: 'Bye, Kim, Bye!' I utter hopefully. The dog looks up at me – and laughs. I wave my arms at him and raise my voice. No reaction. Baby starts crying again and I think there is a hole in my welly. After criss-crossing the area irritably, I have the uncomfortable awareness that they are missing! I clamber over the dunes on to the beach. To say I am getting quite warm would be an understatement, but I am fairly confident that an increasing wetness between me and my youngest is not perspiration.

No, they are not on the beach but my eagle eye has spotted clues – a lot of tracks on the sand and other evidence of recent movement. Oh no, they must be up to their old tricks; I'll bet they have gone across the sands, down to the ewes on the next farm. This is bad news. What a predicament! Shall I:

(a) proceed on the long trail, following their footsteps and, on locating the itinerant mob, clap my hands and shout, 'Ladies, come *back*' (no use expecting any help from that fool of a dog) to that wasteland where the boss hasn't fed you for two days and where there is no shelter from anything the foul north wind cares to deliver?

(b) dismiss all further thoughts of them from my mind and lie to the invalid?

(c) collect the reinforcements of our worker and the older children who have recovered, to try and sort it out?

After due consideration, I go for (b). I am sure that, quizz-wise, this classifies me as a timid, shy person, lacking in self-confidence, who would benefit from a course in assertive-ness, 'coward' for short, but somehow, this seems the only way. After all, family comes first . . . doesn't it?

Baby starts crying again as we struggle homewards against the wind, which is increasing in intensity every minute. Fighting against this force, one realises another factor in the 'no snow' question: generally speaking, snow simply blows across the area horizontally.

At last I stagger into the porch, with one wet foot, a wet middle, irritable and exhausted. What a scene greets me. In the kitchen, where the Aga means that it's the warmest place in the house, there they are, congregated round the portable telly, covered in quilts and apparently in a semi-comatose state. As any stockman knows, a sick beast is one thing – and worrying that may be, but a beast getting better is – a nuisance. I try to creep past unnoticed, to change my soggy clothing, not to mention baby's.

'Ah, Mummy, can you get me a drink/Weetabix/a sandwich/a banana?'

'Get it yourself.'

Tearfully, 'Oh, but I'm not *well*.'

Upstairs, the pale face on the pillow flickers into life. Apparently, the sight of his nearest and dearest stripping off all her clothes, including socks, and hurtling them across the room in disgust, leaves him quite unmoved.

'Everything all right?' he asks weakly, at last.

'Everything except us,' I reply, and then begin to itemise the status quo in each field . . . but he has gone to sleep once more.

'Is that you, Veronica? Your sheep are mixed with mine again.'

'I am sorry but. . . .'

'You people don't look after your stock properly. You are not fit to be farmers. You're . . .'

I replace the receiver and leave my neighbour talking into the air. After due consideration, I remove the receiver again. The farmer in this house will not be ill for long, he never is. No one can tend his beloved ladies like he can. They cannot. This is true. What a bad farmer's wife I am!

Things gradually return to normality again, another crisis is past. The farmer rejoins his sheep; the children go back to school.

On a shopping trip, it becomes evident that Seville oranges have arrived. Dash – I had hoped for a bit of a rest. Oh well, I suppose I had better. . . . To the already laden trolley, removing reluctant toddler first, I add polythene bags filled with the bitter fruit. (I recall many many years ago, whilst working as a mother's help for a busy farming family, unpacking the shopping and mistakenly inserting one or two globular orange fruits into the fruit bowl. The first person to discover my mistake was the farmer himself; I was frightened of him *before* the incident. . . .) Now then, I need bags and bags of sugar.

'Going to be busy?' The supermarket check-out girl is a nice lass but at times can irritate.

Although we adults appreciate home-produced preserves – and probably shouldn't – the children much prefer jars of brightly coloured jellied material from the shop. The reason behind afflicting myself with hours of seemingly mindless labour is so that I can present it on the table of the bed-and-breakfast guests . . . good chunky stuff . . . I like everything to be as rustic as possible. When half of them pick out the peel laboriously and leave it at the side of their plates, I ask myself why I bother.

Every year, I swear will be the last. Every year, I embark upon the task with renewed enthusiasm. I find a new labour-saving method. It makes no difference. At the end of the day, the preparation takes hours and leaves the cook cross and sore-fingered. Then, I boil . . . and I reboil. Why doesn't the dashed stuff set? Finally, I am in the position to be able to stand back and survey rows and rows of gleaming jars of speckled amber spread. Perhaps it was worth it after all?

'Pooh – what's that smell?' is the cry when they come in from school.

I am grateful. I really am. Having a husband who does not shoot (thank goodness) means that you are occasionally the lucky recipient of the present of a pair of feathered creatures, one brightly coloured and one not, left hanging in the back porch. In the end, unable to leave them any longer there, I embark upon the transformation – from elegant, beautifully marked birds, to the misshapen mess on the block before me. I tell myself that the reason for my reluctance is that the job goes against my artistic grain. That's *my* story. At last, the object is ready to be consigned to the waiting bag

17

and merciful anonymity of the freezer. Ugh! I know farmers who pluck and dress hundreds of birds every year for the season, and wives are usually incorporated into this activity – a dubious honour in the interest of marital involvement in an increasingly technological age? They deserve medals! If I were not already a vegetarian, this is undoubtedly the course I would follow under such circumstances.

My hair is covered in a greenish-brown material which smells and looks rather like silage; my husband argues that it has more the texture and taint of horse manure. The debate rages on. Under the polythene cap so thoughtfully provided in the pack it all goes. What would we do without polythene bags? This rather dubious ritual is all in the interest of self-beautification, which this particular farmer's wife and mother rarely has either the time or inclination for. The substance in question is called henna and in common with other 'natural' and 'green' (it certainly is green) products of the age, has a certain acceptability and greater popularity than its more slickly packaged cousins. After finally washing it off – and it seems to take ages and gallons of water – I am not totally convinced it was worth it but in view of the impending rare social engagement, I felt some sort of effort was called for.

Yes, we are not social butterflies and therefore an invitation to the party of the year is not to be sneezed at. The logistics of such an outing are tricky. The baby sitter (my mother) has to be sensitively handled to take on the job in the first place and then we have to ensure that sufficient anaesthetic medication is left on hand to produce the necessary state of euphoria, without actually rendering her unconscious. Once this hurdle is past, we make good our escape into smart society for a few hours.

Oh yes, it was worth it, they are all here. Doctors (obviously it would not be in anyone's interest to be either ill or injured within the next twenty-four hours), lawyers, accountants, merchants, artists . . . even farmers . . . are gathered here under the expert handling of host and hostess. Oh yes, I do not feel that 'glittering occasion' would be too exaggerated a description for what we have here tonight – er – I mean, morning.

The farmer is very busy feeding stock within; he is also feeding stock without (in more ways than one). The fifty or so pedigrees are lambing slowly and from time to time, a shivering, wet bundle is inserted into the oven, hopefully to be reunited with its parent after a few hours of 'simmering'. The weather is of course well and truly back to normal now. All signs of snow have completely disappeared, the wind is rattling the windows and doors, not to mention raising the carpet in the sitting room and the lino in the loo.

'How *do* you keep this place warm in winter?' ask our summer bed-and-breakfast guests.

Short laugh. 'We don't.'

February

By February, we are all becoming a bit fed up with winter. Luckily, the days are now lengthening and the garden is slowly springing to life, with the appearance of the yellow aconite under the bushes and the groups of snowdrops. Soon, the narrow tips of other bulbs will be seen daring to penetrate through the cold soil.

'Right, Veronica, sitting trot round the school!'

I am to be found today in a huge converted barn, not long ago host to hundreds of cattle. Now it is empty except for a handful of human hopefuls and their mounts. Thoughtfully angled beams shine down upon us at this still gloomy stage of the year. At our feet, not straw, certainly not slats but the most incredible substance: rubberised sand!

I should imagine that my presence in this small class has raised the average age by about 400 per cent. Two of the other pupils are my own children but, quite honestly, I don't mind being in a children's group. It is more fun.

After one lap of 'sitting trot' round the huge building – I'll swear they have extended it since last week – I can feel every bone in my body vibrating. Still, it must be good for you. Is that a smirk I see on that child's face? The instructress standing in the middle of the school, wrapped in a multitude of sweaters and scarves, smiles brightly and says, 'Good' but then, she always does. Never mind – her encouragement never fails to spur you on. The children are simply 'naturals'. 'I never had the opportunity when I was your age,' I tell them. 'I hope you realise how lucky you are.'

Instead, in advanced middle age (and I know from experience that I shall feel even older tomorrow), here I am, endeavouring to learn the mysteries of the equine art – and 'mystery' it proves to be on occasions.

Diversification is the name of the game and the woman is frequently the key player. The new livelihood of one farmer's wife is the hobby of another. We go to two farms where they have turned back to the horse for their way forward. This one, with the Indoor Equestrian Centre, complete with competent instructor, is for serious stuff. Watch your diagonals! Remember the sequence of the horse's hooves (I never can). And then, steel yourself from time to time for – horror of horrors – what the instructor casually refers to as 'popping' over a few jumps. This is an elating experience – afterwards.

For a lighter, more laid-back approach, we go to another farm, which still looks very much like a farm. No fancy indoor school here. The yard is higgledy-piggledy with hens, of diverse varieties, often with a brood of tiny chicks in tow; then there are cats and dogs, often with offspring too. All this delights the children to such an extent that the horses themselves often stand unnoticed until mounting time. There are of course individual stalls for the horrifyingly huge hunters who look down at us along their aristocratic noses. On the other hand, the poor ponies which have to put up with people like us live largely in the field and can be seen waiting patiently tethered at odd angles all over the shed. I can imagine:

'Hello, Pedro, who have you got today?'

'One of the children, I think. Doesn't usually give me much trouble as long as I plod along. Seems quite satisfied with that. Easily pleased. Who've you got?'

'I am not sure but I've been flapping my ears and I've the nasty feeling it's that fat girl.'

'Oh, God, you don't mean . . .?'

'I do.'

'The one who looks as if she should be on a strict diet of oats and water for a month. Might give her a bit more go, too. She sits there like a great sack, expecting me to do the work. . . .'

21

> *'Why don't you boot her off?'*
>
> *'I don't think I've the strength to shift her. Tempting thought, though, I must admit. . . .'*

What this second place lacks in efficiency and symmetry, it more than compensates with cleanliness and cheerfulness, largely supplied by the grooms and a loyal band of dedicated little girls, all eager to look after their four-legged friends. Instead of a gruelling hour of finding parts of one's anatomy other activities do not reach, *here* you go out for a *hack*. You may go out with Gemma, Laura or Ann but the entire operation is overseen by the diversifying farmer himself.

Now here we have a character. 'We used to do bed-and-breakfast,' his wife once told me, 'and when Charles served, people thought he was quaint.' Yes Charles is quaint. He reminds me of a swan. By this I don't mean to say that he has a long neck, but come to think of it, he has. No, on horseback, he glides along, gracefully, elegantly upright, totally in tune with the unpredictable creature – just like a swan sailing downstream. But, on dry land, he bustles around awkwardly, as if two-footed ambulation were distasteful to him. He greets everyone with equal enthusiasm, his conversation often comprising staccato sentences without verbs, requiring little or no reply. You soon crack the code.

Hello, there seems to be quite a squad of us here today, there often is on a Saturday. 'You are on Speedy,' someone is saying, 'he's got more go.' Oh, dear, too late to change now; she's moved on to someone else.

I am on. The boys look quite chirpy, perched on their ponies below me. Age changes all. I have a quick look round our companions. There seem to be another two young children, plus father, as well as three or four older children who have that look on their faces which has an uncomfortable effect on a cautious matron taking out her precious offspring. Then there are one or two others who look almost as frightened as I feel. We are to be taken out by Charles himself, the groom informs me with a grin, or is it a sneer?

'You look a little apprehensive, Veronica,' she says.

Apprehensive? 'No, no,' I squeak. Terrified, if you really want to know.

Too late to dismount now. We seem to be moving out. The stirrup-shortening and girth-tightening ceremony is over. I lean down and give Speedy's neck a reassuring pat, with the promise of Polos on our return. You look after me and I'll look after you, kid. You scratch my back and I'll scratch yours – no, that's not right – I do not want those great hooves anywhere near *my* back at any time, thank you.

Yes, I have a neck strap. I must take a deep breath and whistle a happy tune or something because 'they' can sense fear, it is said. 'Don't be frightened and you won't fall off,' is one of Charles' more loquacious pieces of advice.

As we trot together along the road, Charles moves his elegant mount backwards and forwards along the ride, having a word with each. I hear him say: 'Yes, we'll soon go into a field and have a jolly good gallop. . . .'

Before you could even try to say 'Na – ow', the party swings into the said field and after a few words about those who do not wish to gallop staying at the back, behind Gemma, the enthusiasts are off. I position Speedy, trembling, behind Gemma, but here Speedy thinks differently. With a few gleeful strides and a toss of the head, this reluctant jockey is up with the leaders.

This seems to be a situation over which I have little or no control. Everyone seems to be standing in their stirrups, crouched over the horse's neck. I pass two (I didn't want to) on whose faces there is now an expression of what can only be described as total ecstasy. I speed past my eight-year old, his face expressionless as usual. He has never galloped before, poor lamb, is he all right?

'Did you see that rabbit, Mummy?' he cries, removing one hand from the reins to indicate the departing animal.

As the gradient grows steeper, the horses run out of steam and even this inexperienced novice detects the lowering of a gear. Relief is a much under-estimated emotion. Oh-oh, there goes a riderless horse – and another! No, not one of my babes

I hope – I daren't look round. Ah, it is apparently the other two, but Charles has jumped off his own horse, caught theirs and plonked them back on again, recapturing his own before we finally reach a complete halt at the top of the hill.

We walk sedately through the gate, one at a time, on to the road. 'Can we go into another field, mister?' is the cry from a recently unseated rider. Are they quite sane?

How I recall the words of a farmer's wife I knew many years ago, before I was married: 'Never – never – go in for chickens or anything like that, Veronica.' Of course, this was a lady who had no need to eke out her income in any way, who was sitting pretty on her own nest, from which her chicks had flown at an early age, to public school, etc. I often wish I had heeded this advice – not that they bring in much cash anyway. They range free, an activity much beloved of 'green' people but perhaps they do not see their feathered friends foraging in dustbins in winter or pulling out seedlings in spring. Then, we have to buy in food for them, irrespective of whether they produce the goods or not, and this winter, with its cold snaps, has necessarily depressed yields. . . .

What they do do is provide this farmer's wife with a social life, which is not to be sniffed at. I tote eggs round the town to the dwellings of selected dames, most of whom are mad as hatters – perhaps 'eccentric' would be a kinder description – but who are all united in their common desire for my dark golden free-range yolks.

Here is Gwendoline. What *is* she wearing this morning? Her enviably thick black tresses are piled high on her head; her eye make-up is perfect, she was an actress of course. She is wearing a creation in purple which seems to start at the shoulders and pour in torrents to somewhere just above the ankles – ah, there are her arms. I can just imagine this worn with wellies, brushing against the nettles en route to the hen house!

'Darling!' (Why do actors always have such deep voices?

Do they have deep voices and because of them, decide to become actors – or do they develop them on the way?) 'You look marvellous this morning, darling.'

Do I really? A quick peek in the car mirror reveals the usual red face of winter atop the anorak and baggy, shapeless jeans worn cleverly to cover an equally shapeless body. I nip nimbly to the rear of the car where nestle boxes of eggs amongst the baler twine, discarded sweet papers and –

'Want out! Want out!' wails somebody from the back seat. Yes, I bet you do. I know that Dylan has some lovely toys but why doesn't he draw on the wallpaper and break ornaments like ours do? It is all a question of stocking rate, I suppose.

I have to take the under-fives everywhere at the moment as 'Daddy' is so very busy. Kevin, our worker, is still off, so the farmer has to do all the feeding inside, and the outside stock are on the receiving end of increased rations too. Off he goes each morning in his heated cab with Radio 4 nicely tuned – quite a pleasant little trip I should say.

This morning, however, something special is on. The air is filled with raised voices of protesting woolly ladies-in-waiting, as they are at the stage of requiring certain treatments. As a result of life in this technological age, they receive so many injections that you wonder how they could possibly dare to die – ever. But die they do – when they decide to do so – and don't we all know it.

Today it is a combined serum and worming dose. They are gathered together in the big pen, where they are to be found in small groups, complaining and comparing symptoms. Some are fitter than others; some are becoming very fat; it is just as well the weather is quite cold as these woolly coats could get a body down. One by one, they are called, encouraged by a snappy figure in black and white:

'Not much time to discuss problems here – just like a conveyor belt these days – here we go – there he is with his needle – ouch – and back we go to the other pen. One simply

is not treated with respect these days. . . . Still we girls have a few cards up our sleeves; we can still keep the upper hand you know. Some shameless hussies of our acquaintance went to see Roland when he broke into our field in September and haven't they set the cat amongst the pigeons for his lordship. This has meant that he has had to make extra journeys down to the field bringing mums and babes back to base these last few days! Ha — good for them, I say!'

We have a bright pink plastic mouse, holding a wedge of cheese in an equally horrendous shade of yellow; there is a small key at the side and, on turning it, the creature executes a series of backward somersaults. It is quite amusing really, well for the first and second time anyway. However, it suddenly crosses my mind that if only I had a scientific/mechanical mind I could leave it out at night, programmed to be activated at the approach of the real thing. Surely such a confrontation would convince any self-respecting rodent of the error of his ways, and send him squeaking with terror from the scene for ever.

Talk about the patter of tiny feet — as I sit in the kitchen in the middle of the night, nursing a sore ear or head or something (not mine) I can hear them; there seem to be hundreds scuttling up and down the shelves. They chew the newspaper; they penetrate packets I have inadvertently left out prior to emptying the contents into jar, tin or plastic tub. I simply cannot keep ahead of them. They are driving me insane. It seems quite monstrous that the only piece of 'poetry' I can find relating to the species of which I am a part, seems to be biased rather in favour of the animal.

Anyway, I have tried 'humane' traps, which proved exceptionally humane in that they caught nothing. I have tried traps impregnated with scent supposedly attractive to mice but undetectable to the human nose: these were more aesthetically pleasing but useless. I have tried the conventional, old-fashioned wood and wire ones, baited with cheese — and these have worked on many occasions. However, escapes have frequently been made from such a scene of execution, the unfortunate leaving behind a leg or a foot. The prognosis for mouse amputees is poor and the resultant corpses have eventually been found in varying degrees of decomposition in inaccessible spots, e.g. inside dishwasher, washing machine, Hoover. . . . Cats have come and gone; decisions have been reached that we would prefer to deal with mouse 'mischief' rather than that of a cat. . . . I once read in a magazine that a gadget which emitted a noise objectionable to mice could be purchased for a modest sum, but then, I lost the magazine.

'I saw him talking to the fishermen on the beach,' says Jack worriedly on the 'phone. 'The exchange seemed a little acrimonious.' He's good with words is Jack; it is a pity he wasn't so good with fish and then he wouldn't have sold off all the salmon fishing rights on the beach to some unsavoury characters from the town.

Oh – oh, here he comes. 'Er what happened, er, dear?' I begin nervously.

'Those bloody fishermen. I've had enough. I really have. We have put up with them making a mess on the beach with their caravans, tractors, boats, you name it, but Wayne Parkes – he's the worst – has persistently gone through the footpath beside the holiday cottage with his vehicles and churned it all up; on top of that, he shouts abuse at the holiday makers. He is a bad lot. So, I decided this season to start off on a proper footing. I have moved his nets – there's another thing, he just leaves them lying on the ground all winter, with other rubbish, down on the beach, away from the footpath and the cottage. But, do you know what?'

'Calm down, dear. Er – what?'

'He says he is going to sue *me* for damage to *his nets*!'

Fortunately we have a pretty good relationship with the local police force as Wayne is as good as his word.

Suddenly, the kitchen is full of strange crackles and whistles, with the occasional recognisable word. The owner of the pocket to which these noises seem to be traced is entirely oblivious to them. The job in hand at the moment is the taking down of a statement from the defendant, accused of damaging nets known to be already disintegrating. However ludicrous this all is, it seems to take hours, the children have to be amused and kept reasonably quiet and the shepherd's pie burns to a crisp.

P.C. Jones is not crisp. He is a jolly, red-faced man (you could imagine his rendering of that old favourite 'The Laughing Policeman' when he'd had a few), his brass buttons straining over his ample form. When he finally snaps his notebook shut with a flourish, he does not seem in any rush to return to the local hub of police activity.

'Do you remember old so-and-so? Do you remember when he . . .? And then he ran off with whatsit's wife . . . you know, her that was a Jamieson or was it a Williamson before she was married?'

At last he takes his leave. 'Who is winning?' asks a young family member. The 'fight' goes on – for the moment.

We are self-contained in our large house with our large family in this isolated spot. It is a funny place to farm, some might say. Yes, well the hub of the matter – as far as the farmer's wife is concerned anyway – is that it's a funny place to position a farmhouse. True, the road past goes nowhere but we would like to be able to see it for ourselves.

The road is to the east of the house between it and the sea, and a lot of people go past in summer, looking for Holy Island. Unless they want to risk their cars and necks, they are advised to return to the A1, and have another go at it further down the coast. People will argue with you on this subject. Saint Cuthbert and his mates may have done it but I doubt if they were driving a shiny new Ford Sierra at the time. No, I have often thought of doing *teas* for the masses of people who turn their cars round outside the house. . . .

Anyway, the fact is that, generally speaking, we live in a kitchen, which is cool and airy in summer and warm and cosy in winter – but it faces north and the only view from its windows is out on to the classic courtyard, across to the tumbledown garages and stables; thus, we turn inwards on ourselves. The windows at the front of the house at least look over to the distant hills. This privilege is limited to the bed and breakfast guests in summer and no one in winter, as it is simply too darned cold to sit around looking out of the windows. The effect therefore can be a trifle troglodyte in the winter months of the year.

Bearing all these facts in mind, we welcome characters from the outside world who impinge on our life from time to time. Of course, I don't mean the regular visits from fertiliser rep, vet or grain merchant. No – a case in point is Samson the builder and his sidekick. Our fireplace is falling to pieces; Samson does all the builderwork on the estate and finally agrees to come down and do the job for us. Samson is a mountain of a man, his strength is legendary, his head covered with thick dark curls. He surely must use reinforced ladders – even they wobble alarmingly as he treads up them, rung by rung, with purposeful, solid slowness. His mate waits below, rolling a cigarette philosophically. However, today, there are no ladders in the sitting room, where they are now crouched over the fireplace.

'Have you any eggs to spare, Mrs F?' enquires Samson, with an exaggeratedly casual air, as he peers up the chimney.

'No – sorry. Some of them have gone off in all this cold weather we had.' Samson is quite convinced that our eggs have aphrodisiac qualities. This forms the backbone of one of his many theories. He substantiates the claim by indicating our large family. On his last job here, which lasted some time, he bought dozens; even his assistant could not help but be infected by his enthusiasm and he doesn't even like eggs. Samson is triumphant today because he has just heard that Mary at the next-door cottage is 'in the family way' after many childless years; he is quite convinced it is the eggs he exhorted her to eat that have brought about this happy state of affairs. To the best of my knowledge, I don't recall her ever eating any of our eggs but it would be a pity to spoil Samson's story, wouldn't it?

Samson heaves himself up from the fireplace and rolls a cigarette with enviable skill and speed, and strikes a match, illuminating his good-humoured, weatherbeaten features. 'I'll tell you something . . .' he begins, and so starts another of Samson's sagas. This is it. Once folk have finally installed themselves down here, off the beaten track, there is no point in rushing away, is there?

The Aga has gone out. Now, this is serious. I do have an old electric cooker which takes over when we turn off our old friend in summer, so actual cooking can be taken care of, but of course it does not provide the heat and comforting presence. We all know what this means. It means that we have to summon Bert, the plumber/heating engineer. Now, although Samson is certainly larger than Bert, he pales into insignificance when it comes to telling a tale. Between the two of them, we learn much about local life in general and farmers in particular.

'Mr Jones is not available at the moment . . . would you please leave your name and. . . .' so drones the answering machine in its slowly and precisely articulated Yorkshire vowels. Some persons in this house have been known to leave not-very-polite messages after the short pause. Now, *I* do them – a lot of 'would-you-mind's' and 'I-know-you're busy's' and 'when-you-have-time's' usually do the trick. Mind you, he has been promising us a new and more efficient, not to mention economic, central heating system for ages. We actually went ahead and ordered it, 'fired' with enthusiasm, and parts of it now stand in boxes gathering dust in the back kitchen beside the old one. The effect is hardly attractive but we live in hope and we are not houseproud. However, the Aga is a separate issue. What we have here is an acute emergency – as opposed to a chronic condition.

Here he comes, not removing his cap as he enters; Bert rarely removes his cap. 'Bye, it's bloody cold tonight.'

Exactly – and it's cold in the kitchen too – that's the problem, get on and fix it you silly old . . . but no, we know better. This tack gets us nowhere. There is no rushing Bert.

'Haven't had a cup of tea since 7 o'clock this morning,' he grumbles.

'Never stopped . . . been up to er-you-know-what-do-you-call-its – them that has the pigs outside – smell 'em miles off. . . .'

'Do you mean . . .?'

'Aye, that's it. And no sooner had I fixed *their* boiler – he's a smart-Aleck is young Peter – thought he could do it himself you know – what a mess of it he'd made – his wife was pleased to see *me* I can tell you – than his mother phones and wants me to go and look at hers – and you know where *she* lives. . . .'

'Would you like a cup of tea, Bert?'

'Oh, aye – I don't mind.'

'It's been off since first thing this morning. I don't know why. . . .'

'I've been bad this winter – 'flu' – never had anything like it . . . knocked me for six I can tell you . . . couldn't move from my bed for two weeks and couldn't speak for six. . . .'

(So there is justice in this world after all.)

'. . . and I'm not right yet. Couldn't keep a thing down for weeks . . . no appetite, even now. . . .' He leans his rotund body against the Aga and opens his baccy pouch. The younger contingent adore Bert for some reason; they watch his every move in dumb fascination – from filling his pipe to his slow, methodical removal of the innards of the old cooker, cleaning and replacing.

However, Bert does not do anything rash like begin work yet. Oh no, first we have to go through his entire symptomatology for this bug which dares to penetrate his more-than-adequate body defences. Then he moves on to an update of his family – a lengthy and complex saga. Meanwhile, I go back and forth, continuing with what chores I feel able to perform in the chill air. I have found, from experience, that I can leave the kitchen altogether, do something at the other end of the house and on my return, find Bert poised, pipe in hand, waiting to continue his tale at the point I left the room.

At last, hurray, the job is done. We have to wait a while for the cast-iron monster to heat up and warm the room again but the quiet, comforting rumble of the flames inside gives us hope.

Who wants to come and stay in an isolated stone cottage, without central heating, on the Northumbrian coast in February? The telephone rings. 'We are birdwatchers and we'd like to come to your cottage for a long weekend.'

'Er . . . O.K. . . . er, I mean – super.'

A day or two of bustling around, sweeping, dusting and de-cobwebbing ensues. The cottage has been empty since the theatre company. Brrrr . . . the place feels cold, put on the heaters. It feels warmer outside.

On the day of their arrival, I light the fire downstairs and the woodburning stove upstairs. (Great selling points these – gets 'em back to basics: combing the beach for driftwood; thereafter sitting in the warm glow resulting from their own endeavours in the knowledge that the best things in life are free. Some cheat and use coal or, worse still, rely on heaters, for which of course they pay by means of meter.) Anyway, at last the place is ready, warm and welcoming. I await the arrival of the woolly-hatted, kagooled and heavy-booted birdwatchers. Ah – there goes the door. I will not say 'the bell rings' for the bell broke long ago and what remains is a noise faintly reminiscent of a constipated frog.

There he stands. 'Is this Goswick Farm?'

We really should have a sign or something. 'Yes, er . . .?'

Not quite what I had expected. A young, rather handsome face beneath a carefully styled mass of thick dark hair; he is wearing a T-shirt, jeans and trainers. Oh dear. He has obviously just stepped out of a well-heated car, where sits his female counterpart, combing her hair, looking decidedly unimpressed. Birdwatchers? I give them the key with every expectation that they will be back within ten minutes, hot-foot for the nearest hotel. But, no, the minutes tick by. I relax.

Next morning, as the farmer returns from his rounds at about 11.30 am he observes *all* curtains of the house still tightly drawn. The situation remains unchanged at 3 pm when he goes past with a big bale for the cows. The occupants are not sighted at all. The same happens the following day, the day of departure in fact.

At about 4 pm, the birdwatcher arrives at the house, complete with key, and in reply to the polite question, announces that they have had a lovely weekend, thank you, and do we have any brochures he can circulate amongst his friends? Is this a new facet to the listed qualities of the cottage, hitherto described as a haven for ramblers, birdwatchers, naturalists of all kinds, those with dogs, those with children. . . . A love nest? Why not?

No sooner have I cleared up the mess the 'birdwatchers' left when I receive a call from some students at Newcastle University. Could a party come up for the weekend? What is going on in the world? On arrival, the party in question comprises an assortment of races and creeds, united under the umbrella of the course they are studying: 'Management of the Tropical Coastline'.

The world definitely *is* going mad. Even in summer, you could hardly describe this coast as anything but cool. The weather varies from the January siege to mildish, but of one thing you can be certain, it will be windy most of the time. This weekend is no exception; in fact, I have to admit that 'windy' is not the word. It is gale-force one minute, storm-force the next and blasts of even 100 mph are apparently recorded. Small wonder there are few trees around. The animals here become accustomed to it, the cattle turning their backs to the wind and waiting for their bales and better weather, the sheep spread out amongst the dunes, taking what shelter they can find.

On Sunday morning, the usually cheerful shiny brown face of a young Filipino is transformed with horror as the farmer hails him cheerfully on his way past. On departure, they lean against the wind as they load their cars and thankfully pile themselves into it.

'Are you going straight back to the town or are you stopping off sightseeing on the way?' I ask, pocketing the cash before it blows away.

'Does it matter?' the burnished brown face (tinged with blue) replies. 'Anywhere must be better than this.'

I see.

At the end of February comes half-term, when this farming family, in common with many others, used to head for the sun for their annual holiday. However, once the head count exceeded four, even this escape was abandoned and now we receive visitors here instead. This week, we have an enthusiastic family from London in the cottage. I never worry about Londoners, they always love it here. They appreciate the isolation, lap up the simple lifestyle, marvel at the quiet roads, and adore the absence of the telephone and all the trappings of modern society. They never notice the curling wallpaper, temperamental cooker . . . the cold. . . .

This family is mercifully no exception. He wears a beard, is 'in computers' and his letter of confirmation was written on recycled notepaper – I know we can relax. At the end of the week, they depart, having had a wonderful time, as expected. I muck out the place with the aid of No. 1 Son, the incentive being (in addition to his statutory fixed rate for the job), *finds*.

His obsessive inquisitiveness is harnessed to good use as no stone is left unturned. Inside drawers, under wardrobes, behind cupboards – every inch is searched meticulously. On this occasion, his luck is in. The booty at the end of a highly comprehensive search comprises: the cassette tape of a John le Carré novel, the cassette tape of an obscure pop singer, an empty cassette container, the contents of which would have been slightly more promising, a sock, a safety pin and – a dog turd under one of the beds. This last item I could have managed quite nicely without but the finder seemed quite unmoved; no doubt he was still propelled by the excitement generated by his former gems.

Yes, I am glad that, despite the additional work (much more than in summer, due to the fires and accessories generally associated with winter living) people *do* come to the holiday cottage in winter. It wakes both the house and me from the turgid state of winter hibernation, not to mention easing the diminishing winter cash flow.

Meanwhile, the farmer is, of course, busy with his constant to-ing and fro-ing in the fields, laden with food for hungry mouths. He loves it, whatever the weather. Admittedly, there can be nothing like closing the heavy farmhouse door on the rain, wind or snow and coming into the cosy warmth of the kitchen.

March

This may be the first month of spring, but it still strikes an icy blast into the heart of many a farmer's wife. March means lambing. I sit on the fence and think about it. On one side, everyone – and someone in particular – becomes very tired. Tempers become a trifle short, and the whole process seems to take so *long*, what with the run-up and the run-down. . . . On the other side, of course, life becomes very basic – back to nature and all. Routine domestic tasks can be pushed aside, and furthermore, the whole family can join in, unlike many other farming activities of today. Whether this workforce is as welcome as it is willing is another matter!

One definite *plus* for March is the welcome return of Kevin, our worker. He is overjoyed to be back too. He has spent most of the winter winkle picking (weather permitting) and looking after his children whilst his wife worked. In short, he is worn out and glad to get back to the farmwork familiar to him. Kevin is young, fit, strong and able; he cheerfully carries out any agricultural or horticultural task given to him.

His wife, Evelyn, works for me in the house two mornings a week. They have two children at school and the baby she complacently trundles round from their cottage when Kevin is working. Kevin is quiet but Evelyn has a nice line in home-spun philosophy, which does not come between her tasks. We are very lucky. Evelyn volunteered to help me after the birth of – er – one of our children and I have kept her on and on. I couldn't manage without her. Well, I could, of course I could, but why should I? I daresay 'someone' could manage without Kevin too.

I do feel a bit guilty at times; Evelyn is a severe asthmatic –

as are her children – but she is so anxious not to let me down (she knows what a mess the place would soon be in without her) and she staggers round whatever condition she is in. It is a little disconcerting that instead of having a cup of coffee and a fag mid-morning, Evelyn gaspingly hooks herself on to the nebuliser (breathing machine) on occasion.

Two of our children are asthmatics too. There seems to be a lot of it about these days. Some say of course that it is all the chemicals used to spray the crops . . . the debate will go on. Whatever the reason – and I suspect that the answer is a complex one – Evelyn and Kevin are invaluable.

We are all geared up preparing for the lambing. Pens are being put up in the shed. I find it fascinating, ignorant female that I am, that each year the arrangements differ slightly from the year before; there is always some new refinement he has thought of. It is all good stuff. New thoughts and ideas must constantly flow. Time does not stand still, does it? We have around four hundred mules and a hundred and fifty Black-faces. The ewes receive yet another needle in their rumps at the antenatal clinic:

'Surely this is the last, dear. I couldn't bear another one. I don't think he is as careful as he used to be. These needles aren't sterile, and that last one seemed not only blunt but rather on the rusty side too; I am quite glad I kicked him on the shin.'

'Well, not long to wait now, darling. Is this your first? Oh, second. Oh well, you know all about it then. Did you have a bad time last year? Oh you poor dear – he didn't? A breech can be nasty – and then you lost one? I do sympathise. I don't like to boast but I am coming up to my seventh. Surely my last you say. Well, I cannot think how I have kept going for so long. I have looked after myself of course.

'Mind you, some of the Blackies are even older but then they are different. They aren't like us, dear. Don't mix you know. Ah well, I shall be just as pleased when it's all over this time, the old legs aren't what they used to be. Mind

you, I do get fed up with these medics marvelling about my age – they do make a song and dance about it these days. You are supposed to fit into a category, according to age, weight, and so on (I blame computers) and woe betide you, if you don't. You are a freak! There is only one thing – I take comfort in the fact that I know more about the process than they do. Anyway, at all events, I am quite looking forward to admission. In the shed it is nice and cosy – and meals are brought to you at regular intervals. . . . Can't be bad, can it?'

Oh yes, we are really getting things organised this year. Another innovation is the postnatal field. The untidy patch of grass outside the farm has been fenced off for this very purpose. I know it's an excellent idea but I am blowed if I see why I should marvel at it enthusiastically every time I go past it. The plan is that mums and babes should rest here for a day or two, getting used to each other – *bonding* is the word – and the weather, prior to the long trek forward to the field.

At present, the area lies empty, being eyed by cockerel and his favourite lady friends. They are unmoved by all the fuss as they have been raking through the rough grass for years. Perish the thought but probably many an old egg will turn up with all the trampling and grazing. Ugh! Probably, with the new fencing, this area will become even more attractive to the poultry population, like the garden.

'Hey, girls, I don't think they want us in here any more. What fools! As if a few flimsy strands of wire could keep us out. Over we go! Oh, are you going under? You don't think you could manage flying this morning? Well, it's six and two threes; easy-peasy!'

Whilst all this activity is taking place outside, the farmer's wife has other things on her mind inside. She does not go in for spring cleaning as such, but major upheavals of drawers and cupboards seem appropriate.

Why on earth did I keep these? Surely no one will ever

wear that poofy outfit Mother brought back from Hong Kong! Embroidered hearts, I ask you! The black plastic bag is bulging. All this is the result of having a large house and large family: clothes are passed down from pile to pile or, if they are lucky, drawer to drawer. Finally, you are left with a heap of unworn rejects because it is amazing how discerning (and forcibly so) even a three-year-old can be – aided by the snide sniggers of older siblings of course.

Then there is the sympathy syndrome; those with conventionally sized families rarely wear their clothes actually out: 'I know – we'll pass them on to the Fraters – poor souls – such a large family. . . .' Now, don't get me wrong, I am very grateful for these gifts, I really am. As a result of them, in fact, I rarely actually have to buy garments. However, it means that we usually find we have a surfeit in some areas: the pile of trousers-for-two-year-olds topples into the T-shirts.

And don't they have weird designs on T-shirts these days? The boys put their muddy feet firmly down, refusing to wear garments depicting 'Care Bears' or 'My Little Pony'. Now, those boldly embellished with Transformers, Dennis the Menace or even an old Massey Ferguson will be worn until the pattern is hardly discernible, the neck is coming unstitched and the sleeves are trying to part company with the body.

We soldier on with this seemingly insurmountable task, the operation halting when those present gleefully pounce upon a selected garment. Who says only girls like dressing up? Oh no – they have mixed my 'ins' with my 'outs' again!

At last, wearily I draw up on the double yellow lines outside the charity shop and stagger over the threshold, laden with my bulging bags. The elderly ladies officiating regard me over their glasses with an expression of mingled gratitude and exasperation. I can read their minds: 'Oh, it must be *that* time of year again. It's that odd woman from the country, you know the rubbish *she* brings in.' They say, 'Oh, thank you, dear – how kind – lovely – I wonder – would you be most awfully kind and carry it through to the back? Thank you so much, dear. Are you off? Goodbye! Oh – I see – yes, do have a look around.'

Yes, I have forgotten the yellow lines and screaming kids. I have just thought of something.

'Do you have any sports jackets?'

Yes, the time has come to purchase the lambing jacket – a disposable item bought each year at this time. No, I think, even for lambing, he will reject that one bearing the tartan of the Royal Hunting Stewart – or the one with the bold orange and purple checks. Did anyone ever actually wear it I ask myself?

What it really comes down to is size. This farmer, although he claims he sheds pounds and pounds during lambing – and I don't dispute this – can afford it. Hmmm, this one looks OK, a rather tasteful heather shade in tweed. Yes, the seams look strong, the lining is intact, there are plenty of roomy pockets without holes, designed for the secreting of syringes, rubber rings, bottles. . . . Yes, this looks like the very thing – all for the princely sum of two pounds. I'll take it.

The car is still there, mercifully not displaying a fluttering pink ticket; the wardens must be elsewhere. The kids look accusingly at me from grubby, tear-stained faces: 'You've been *long*.'

The lambing slowly trickles to a start. Insidiously, it creeps up and just as you are beginning to relax, thinking that it's not going to be so bad this year – *pow* – you are thrown into a series of catastrophes and dramas and then, the gruelling, grim, lambing proper settles over us like dust for the duration.

It is late. He is just putting on his overalls prior to making his late night rounds, with the usual 'Who's had the torch this time?' and 'Have you seen the powdered milk?' followed by much clanking and swearing in the sink. Now then, every mother knows that a child throwing up is no rare occurrence but this infant somehow manages to cover two beanbags, about ten square yards of floor, himself and his mother in the process. Every mother also knows that two pairs of hands are better than one on such occasions. But, no, one pair is already on the latch of the door. Suddenly the exit ritual in the back kitchen has changed up a gear and he is out of the door like a shot.

By the time he returns, the washing machine is merrily whizzing round its second load, the kitchen smells like the casualty department at the hospital (we have had plenty of opportunities for comparison) and the patient is lying peacefully asleep, unaware of all the work he has caused his weary parent.

However, there is justice in the world outside, trouble at shed – a difficult presentation over which he has sweated for hours. There is nothing for it, the vet has to be called. More buckets disappear, together with towel and good soap (how often does it reappear with straw and less edifying material adhering to it – if it reappears at all?) I decide it is time to retire and exhaustedly climb the stairs several times with diverse loads: sick child, baby, tray of night-time drinks and medicines. . . .

Just as I am at last leaving the kitchen for the last time, he comes back, worn out. Alistair the vet was tired too and none too pleased to be called out to this far-flung outpost of his practice just as he was blissfully counting sheep between the sheets. Even he had problems with this lambing. Outcome: both lambs dead; mother not far behind. Suddenly, he spies a cardboard box on the floor, brought in earlier. 'Why didn't you put it in the oven?' he explodes.

'The box wouldn't fit,' I wail weakly, 'so I gave the lamb a hot water bottle instead.' Thunderously, he thrusts the lamb, box, hot water bottle and all into the oven, the cardboard box collapsing in the process.

The next morning, the lamb is dead and I feel like joining it.

Yes, I am on the receiving end of the occasional strange

look from the supermarket check-out girls.

'Do you want a box?'

'Yes – er – I'll have that one – er, no, *that* one. Should be the right size for putting lambs in the oven.'

The assistant smiles nervously and thinks: 'Of course, she's not quite right; couldn't be anyway to have had all those children. . . .'

'I think, before the season really gets under way this year, we'll have to have some decorating done, both here and at the cottage.'

'I'll ask Fred up the road to come down, if you like. He is not working at the moment.'

Fred comes down and inspects the work to be done in his usual unenthusiastic way.

'Course, I hate decorating,' he remarks after a while to no one in particular.

'But I thought you said you'd do odd jobs of any kind? You did your own place, didn't you?'

'Oh – don't worry – I'll do it. It's just that I don't *like* doing it that's all.'

It crosses my mind that I don't actually *like* washing, ironing, cooking, cleaning, changing nappies, washing dishes – but if I were being paid by the hour for doing them. . . .

I smile brightly at Fred and offer him a cup of tea.

'It's not poof's tea, is it – like that last time I came here?'

'It's all right, Fred, I'll give you a tea bag from the bed-and-breakfast department.' Anything to please him.

'Yes, I'll do it – I'm not very quick though – and I'll only be able to come odd hours as I've got something else on at the moment.'

'What's that?'

'Gardening.'

'Do you *like* gardening?'

'No, I hate it.'

We soon get into the swing of things, despite all the adversity, and Fred progresses well, starting with the house.

'You know, it's like Blackpool Illuminations here,' he grumbles over his tea bag. 'Doesn't anyone turn off a light?'

We give him a free rein when it comes to colour. It is the B-and-B department he is tackling of course. As long as the finished effect is fresh and clean, and not too fierce, I am happy. Fred has great delight, therefore, in mopping up all the cheap offers at the paint shop. He likes a bargain does Fred. And although he would never admit it, coming from his very orderly household of two children and obedient working wife, he quite enjoys the chaos and the noise.

'It reminds me of Butlins, here!' he declares.

Eventually, he moves on to the cottage and this is where his free rein, combined with this week's special offer, are his undoing. I pop in one afternoon, to have a chat and marvel at his progress. What a shock greets me in the upstairs lounge.

'God Almighty! What colour do you call this?'

I thought he twitched a bit as I came up the stairs. The bright orange walls seem almost to collapse on top of me and – with the lime green woodwork, the effect is . . . well, startling.

'It grows on you after a while,' says Fred, lacking his usual confidence.

God forbid. I walk out and blink and then, walk in again. No.

'But you said I could do what I liked,' he wails.

'Yes, Fred,' I begin soothingly, 'but your previous choices have been so tasteful. . . .'

Fred decides that the time has come to take on reinforcements, and his poor, long-suffering wife, Jane, is brought in to assist the completion of the 'contract'.

Over two tea bags one evening later in the week, Jane announces that the lounge walls are now the palest of pale greens: 'a hint of a tint'.

I breathe a sigh of relief.

At last all the work is completed well in time for Easter

and Fred comes round, quite pleased with himself, to collect his deserts. The kitchen is full of our family, two extra boys, a friend sitting drinking coffee and Evelyn vainly trying to sweep the floors.

'It's like Piccadilly Circus here,' says Fred.

'Is this Goswick Farm?'

A rather gaunt young woman stands on the step, closely followed by an anaemic-looking young man.

'Oh, you must be. . . .'

'Yes, we've rented your cottage for two weeks.'

'Ah, you're early. Never mind, it's quite ready apart from a mattress in the upstairs bedroom; I've had to buy a new one. My husband will bring it along when he gets back from his sheep. Is that all right?'

'Oh – er – yes.'

They drift away rather than leave, wearing slightly vacant smiles. Are they on something? Oh, well – never mind – I've quite enough to worry about without wasting my time pondering the welfare of holiday cottage occupants.

Back he comes in better mood – the shed is running more smoothly this morning, thank goodness.

'By the way, dear; there is that mattress to go along to the cottage.' To my relief he smiles and says he'll take it along straight away. The lambing must be going well.

A short time later.

'You'll never guess what?'

'What, dear – sextuplets?'

'No, at the cottage I mean.'

I had quite forgotten that he had turned right instead of left, leaving the house, surely a supreme effort.

'I go in carrying the mattress just as they are going out to see the sights. "Do be careful," they say, "we are practising Buddhists and we've set up our altar." What do you think of that?'

'Fantastic!' What a change not to talk about sheep.

Midweek: 'Mrs Frater – do you think we could have some

more eggs? It's Adrian's birthday and I am baking him a cake!'

'How nice. How old is he?' I ask absently.

'Thirty-three.'

These Buddists are strange.

'Of course,' I begin, 'our eggs have rather spectacular qualities, the builders maintain that they. . . .'

Edwina seems quite unmoved by these claims. Obviously, their lifestyle, altars and all, cannot be improved in any way.

Samson suddenly appears again, a law unto himself. He was supposed to come weeks ago, when the cottage was empty – to perform some sort of operation inside the chimney. He had to come *now* didn't he? Edwina is not very pleased, we understand. Well, I suppose that all that banging interferes with her meditation.

The job does not take long. It is amazing how much more quickly you work when someone is staring at you, trying to transform you into a spider or something by means of rapid exit from and re-emergence into this world. Samson seems to be quite pleased to be out of our orbit – eggs or no eggs!

The lambing must be getting easier for he's gone up to the cottage again this afternoon to inspect Samson's handiwork. The trouble is, he has forgotten his key. They appear to be out. Therefore, he nimbly climbs in through the dining room window (perhaps he is losing weight after all) just in time to give Adrian a fright, bordering on coronary arrest, perhaps speeding *his* departure from the world. No, they weren't out, merely having an afternoon sleep. Well, they are on holiday.

I suppose that now is the time to turn to thoughts of the garden. It is an unfortunate law of nature that most farmhouses sit in an acre or so walled into this category. It is a recognised (and almost respected) fact that farmers do not like gardening; they have quite enough of the soil and things that live in it to avoid all other contact. It is possible that farmers' wives may have a similar aversion – and would prefer to turn the area in question over to sheep, goats, hens or government set-aside. However, such a course would be severely frowned upon by mother-in-law and might possibly deter the Bee and Bees, on whose income we depend for a large part of the year. Therefore, efforts are made – I think that is an honest and accurate description at this farm.

I find that my horticultural activity occurs in two main bursts – one now, and one in the autumn when all my mistakes are pulled out with the weeds of the season past. In the autumn I may also plant bulbs and plants for next year, spurred by the enthusiastic perusal of catalogues which come plopping through the letterbox. That's one thing about gardening – you are always looking *forward* – little point in looking back. A disaster is a disaster, something to put behind you and learn from. . . .

In the early years in the job, this gardener spent a good deal of time undoing all the work of her predecessor, taking such revolutionary steps as uprooting the floribundas and chrysanthemums. She soon found herself with a predicament – vast tracts of empty soil, in which she has performed a variety of interesting experiments over the years. Trial-and-error, this technique is called, but now, an older and wiser woman, the gardener wishes she had kept the roses.

Anyway, here I am, at the start of yet another year, horticulturally speaking, wondering where on earth to start. Do I start at the bottom, with the digging prior to planting potatoes and other vegetables or do I begin at the house with a little gentle weeding or pruning? It is really a matter of how I feel. Do I want a workout or a gentle stretch? Be bold – Evelyn's here to keep an eye on the children! Resolutely I march down the garden, armed with spade and what I hope is grim determination.

Ten minutes later, puffing, I stand and look back. Is that all I have done? How much more is there to go? Perhaps the children need me . . . perhaps I should . . . don't be pathetic

. . . you *must* finish this patch: *achievement* is the name of the game. At last I straighten up – well, try to straighten up – and walk painfully towards the house.

'The children are fine. You've time for a bit more gardening.' These are not the words I want to hear. I sow my sweet peas on the kitchen windowsill instead.

'It's Mother's Day today. You should be resting and Daddy doing all the housework for you . . . and the cooking . . . and looking after us and. . . .'

'Don't be silly, dear. Daddy's busy with the lambing.'

'No, he isn't. He's sitting reading the papers.'

'Oh.'

To be honest, he did buy me some toffee from the baker's van. The fact that I haven't eaten toffee for years, due to dental problems, does not devalue the deed, does it? He ate it himself – and I hope he has toothache.

No, I couldn't say that Mothers' Day is any different from any other. Never mind, it's not all bad. Sitting on the sideboard is a lovely painted daffodil, contrived from a piece of egg carton – a present from play school.

Oh – oh, things are returning to normal outside.

'What's the matter, dear? Would you like a cup of coffee?'

'Bloody things. No logic in their behaviour. You simply can't win.'

Who on earth can he be talking about I ask myself?

'This ewe I told you about. . . .'

'Did you, dear . . . ?' Sugar, butter, milk – what else do I need? Why do I have to make so many shopping trips? Most farmers' wives only shop once a week. Mind you, I am often quite glad to get away from you know what.

'What was that, dear?'

'You know – that mule who refused to take her own lambs. I have had her in the adopter box for about three weeks and. . . .'

'Not three *weeks*, surely?'

'Well – ages.'

'What has happened?'

'I tried taking them out again. This time, to my relief, she took them – suddenly seemed quite fond – complete change of character. I left them in the pen, intending to put them out when I had finished my other jobs. When I went back . . . she had dropped down *dead*.'

'Oh dear.'

'I wasn't very pleased – and neither were her lambs.'

'I'm not surprised. What on earth did she die of? Heart attack? Stroke?'

'Does it matter? She is dead and now I've got to find someone to look after the lambs. Blessed things. You never know where you are with them.'

'Mrs Frater?'

'Yes.'

Two eager young men stand on the step, clad in raincoats a darker shade of pale.

'Detective Sergeant Smith and Detective Constable Watt. May we come in? We're making enquiries about some people you have staying in your holiday cottage.'

Something clicks in my mind. I have seen a few films. Well, I did a long time ago.

'Can I see your identification cards, please?' I hope I sound suitably confident. I am rather pleased with this.

'Oh, Christ, yes. Silly of me.'

I am suddenly confronted, several inches from my nose, with two monochrome prints of unsmiling faces stuck to cards, proclaiming that the gentlemen in question are amongst those chosen to keep the peace in this country of ours.

'All right. Yes?'

'You have some people staying in your cottage, with the name of Poppletwine or Jones?'

'Er – yes.'

'They have been creating disturbances in estate agents round about – and using different names.'

I suggest to the young officer (I do feel old) that he might switch to the other's name from time to time if he had been blessed with an appendage like Poppletwine.

'Oh – well – er, point taken, Madam. But there seems to have been some erratic behaviour and – his voice lowers and his eyes gleam – 'Irish accents.'

'Irish accents? Don't make me laugh!' (I have always had a dubious feeling about the IQ of estate agents.) 'They're from Glasgow.'

'Oh.' The confident air of the two young policemen, who thought that their hour had come at last (a coup – an IRA cover blown – promotion for sure) is gradually disappearing.

'I see. So – in your opinion, Madam, they are OK?'

'Well, I wouldn't go as far as to say that. They are a trifle *strange* but then, they are practising Buddhists.'

'Practising Buddhists!'

The face of the young detective becomes impassive. He snaps his notebook shut, turns to his colleague and back to me.

'Well, I don't think we need to bother you any more, Madam. Sorry to have disturbed you. Good morning.'

I have to laugh. In our quiet rural existence it is not often we have a thrill like this.

Something moves quickly past me through the kitchen. At lambing time, all actions become olfactory, and you rely less on the other senses, the smell becoming stronger with the passing weeks. On this occasion, it disappears into the office, titivating the nostrils of those remaining in the kitchen. I cannot hear what he is saying on the phone. As I told you, the other senses recede. Here he comes at last, his face grim.

'I am taking the dog to the vet immediately. I have run him over.'

Oh no, not again. Admittedly, the last time was about ten years ago and a different dog. I may say that the dog concerned required a series of expensive operations and was never the same again. He was eventually pensioned off to Cousin John where he subsequently killed himself by running across the path of an oncoming car. Funny old life, isn't it?

Anyway, back to the present. This dog's jaw is broken. I am not very brave, and I look through the window in trepidation. But there he is standing quite cheerfully, looking as if he has a permanent laugh; a bit bloody perhaps, but obviously not in much pain. Off they go, the pair of them, to the long-suffering vet. Only one returns an hour later. The dog is to receive immediate surgery, the prognosis is good.

Today I am going to give myself a treat – strictly in the name of business of course – by abandoning ships (or I should say 'sheep') and attending a sale at the local auction rooms. The children have broken up for the Easter holidays and I have left them at home, largely looking after each other but overseen by the eagle eye of Evelyn. I have the baby in the pram outside. I have already 'viewed'.

Over the years I have learned a thing or two here. It is simply not good enough to wander around regarding items in casual fashion, as in a shop. No, you have the little notebook or catalogue and pencil, and you bend, touch and inspect minutely. If there are moving parts, move them; if it is china, turn it over to see 'the mark'. All these little touches add up to the habitual auction attender. Regrettably, this attender only goes when it is urgent to replace an item of furniture in the house or the holiday cottage, and the 'ceiling' is low.

As I say, I did my homework by nipping in after shopping on Friday; didn't stay long due to the dirty looks from the auctioneer's clerk, watching for sticky fingers and muddy shoes. Here we all are then, waiting for the off. The action is orchestrated so that the cheap stuff goes first, gradually rising in crescendo, with a climax of antiques and objets d'art early afternoon, which gently recedes back down to the rugs and curtains at the end.

Yes, I am in a good spot to see them all, sitting on the assortment of sofas and chairs to be sold – a fair sprinkling of farmers' wives on a similar errand to myself, or perhaps looking for something suitable for the sideboard. There are a few recognisable dealers in the room too, local junk shop owners and some slightly higher up the scale. Ah – there's Agnes, I haven't seen her for ages. I move towards her, carefully squeezing past all shapes and sizes of humanity, and we conduct a conversation in noisy whispers until we receive the frown from the auctioneer.

Jeremy works hard, he really does. There he stands on his rostrum, immaculately turned out and debonair. The ladies love him. Apart from throwing himself body and soul into the sale, he conducts asides with his front row and there are collectors' items of repartee. I have the sneaking suspicion that some of his fans go with no intention of actually purchasing anything at all. All is quiet now, noses are blown and throats are cleared between lots.

Half an hour into the sale and I have spent my cash limit of a tenner on two beds and a couple of electric heaters for the cottage. I operate on the principle that you buy cheap 'disposable' items, not decent stuff to be looked after, patched up and painted at the start of each season. Every spring I assess the situation and replace where necessary. I suppose I should go home now but I am finding it hard to tear myself away, so I stay on.

I wonder what that hideous china cat will fetch? It looks as if it has been overindulging in Whiskas and is embellished with an ornate Eastern design; I would love to buy it for my friend, Elizabeth, who hates cats. Oh-oh, must be getting near lunchtime. Out come the flasks and carefully wrapped packets of sandwiches. I wish I had brought a flask myself, I feel a bit parched. Good grief, fancy that linen basket going for *that*!

Here it comes, the cat. Ha, that's me out. I would have gone up to a fiver (Elizabeth has been a good friend), but I don't believe it – eighty-five pounds! And it is hideous, you must believe it. Now, we come to a lifesize pewter duck, with moving parts which would make a lovely birthday present for you-know-who – especially in the morning, minus his specs, after a heavy night! No, too dear again!

I am going. I feel refreshed now, ready to face anything – all the kids wrecking the place in the early idleness of 'the hols', lambs in boxes, sinks of syringes and stomach tubes. . . .

To the surprise of all members of the family, *he* decides to take some time out mid-lambing too. We are all flabbergasted. After two weeks of all waking hours (and often sleeping ones too) being occupied with woolly creatures, he suddenly announces he will have an early lunch and take himself off to the county NFU Meeting. I know he is the branch delegate but this is a bit rash, isn't it? Deserting your post, and all that? 'Kevin can manage for a few hours.' True.

Overalls are flung on the floor, wellies are kicked aside, and he actually manages to hit the peg with his cap as he tosses it upwards playfully – oops, it's down again. No matter, off he goes in his underpants upstairs, from where we soon hear the rare burr of the razor removing the 'designer stubble', accompanied by whistling. He soon reappears, jauntily jumping down the stairs, two at a time, ducking to avoid the sandwich thrown at him. We are left wondering what to do with the long, wet afternoon, while he is earnestly planning policies and improving the image of the farmer nationwide.

April

'I stopped the car the other day to watch a field of lambs playing. I sat there for ages. Aren't they lovely?'

Eh? Is she quite right? Not a farmer's wife for sure.

I am having my weekly fix of equine therapy again. Actually, talk about lambs does make a change from my companion's lyrical descriptions of her new bathroom colour scheme.

Although where we ride is a farm and I know that there are lambs all around, I stare fixedly between the horse's ears at the road ahead, successfully removing them from my field of vision. I hope we have a gallop, I think to myself as we move slowly away from the farm. This is highly unlikely now as the fields have all been sown and we are restricted to the quiet roads and pathways through the woods. The latter are our destination today, and you really appreciate the leafy glade when you live in a spot devoid almost of all trees apart from the odd bent bush.

The children love the woodland rides but Wednesday is my day and proving relaxing as usual – all woolly thoughts, shopping lists and plans for springtime upheaval have receded as I concentrate on the horse, with one ear cocked for the cheerful chatter of the groom. It is a beautiful day, the sun is shining, spring is in the air, I can smell it. No, I can safely swear that there cannot be a sheep within a radius of at least two hundred yards, now we are in the heart of the wood, cantering smoothly along – well, fairly smoothly. Why has he stopped so suddenly, I gasp, as I almost disappear over his head.

'He is going to the toilet,' is the reply.

These polite little phrases make me laugh, but I suppose they are standard terminology for the needs of the small children who largely comprise the rides. What next? Oh no, you know I don't like jumping. I hate it, I am terrified, and it does upset me to watch 'Bathroom Colour Scheme' gliding gracefully over those fences like a bird. In fact, if you really want to know, it makes me sick. But yes, I did have a nasty experience 'at the other place' last year when I caught my foot in the stirrup as I fell off, spraining my ankle. It has never been the same since. I know I am a coward but it could well be a case of this time ankle, next time a more important bone like skull or spine.

At last, reluctantly, we turn for home. An hour is hardly long enough, but it is really as much as I can spare at this, or any other, time of year. Nevertheless, as I slide lithely (ha) off the warm back, my mind is totally cleared. What is she saying? Oh, she has to dash home to shampoo the cat – she is so busy.

I remove the saddle and bridle from the patient and long-suffering animal and administer the statutory dose of Polos. I never get ten out of ten for hanging up the bridle in the tack-room, and I once put a head collar on to a horse upside down. The poor creature – luckily a particularly gentle soul – looked quite bemused, as well one might, with a strap covering one's eyes.

Then, involuntarily, I allow a white woolly creature to creep into my sight and this triggers off a whole chain of events, past, present and future, associated with lambing. I slowly climb back into the car, remove my hard hat and replace it with the farmer's wife/mother's one and drive home.

We are getting well through the lambing now, but there is still plenty of work for the weary farmer.

I do not ask how it is going (I am not 'involved' on a regular basis like many farmers' wives for obvious reasons). The children do. 'How many left to lamb, Daddy?' goes the cry from various sources three or four times a day. It must be recorded to his credit that he retains his temper at such times, still touched by their interest, poor soul.

With experience, you learn not to look at it in terms of numbers. The 'killer' once you reach this stage of the game is the amazingly frustrating business known as 'mothering up'. At the end of a long day in the shed, even if it has been punctuated by regular injections of tea and coffee, spending hours trudging round a huge field, often battling with the elements, struggling with sheep social work is no joke.

'What number are you?' It is difficult to see with that purple spray – ridiculous colour. Looks like 109 or is it 104? Oh well, the truth is that it is bellowing loudly at the edge of the field with no sign of a brother or a mother, which are undoubtedly together somewhere in this dashed field. Why are there so many ups and downs and bits of bush here and there? I feel certain that in days to come the entire operation will be computerised, or the lambs and their mama will be equipped with neat little bracelets or collars giving off matching signals. The necessity of these wobbly numbers on their backs in hideous hue will be avoided, and hopefully a lot of human time and effort.

In the meantime, we march grimly round, looking for an anxious mother, one child tied to her apron strings, no doubt looking smug and well-fed. 104 or 109 (purple) does not take kindly to being carried unceremoniously under the arm and allows his displeasure to be felt in the usual manner down the side of the jacket. Who cares?

Hello, what about this lady, she seems to have only one child. What is the number? Aha, it could well be 104 or 109, it is certainly purple – eureka! There you are, dear, there's your baby back; I bet you have been worrying yourself silly wondering what had happened to him! Why, you ungrateful bitch, fancy kicking the poor mite like that! You will be reported to the authorities you will and no mistake, and appropriate action taken. What do you do with a miserable matron in a field who flatly refuses to look after her infant? More than that, she actually batters him! However, if you think I am going to stand around in the fast-declining daylight with a bitterly cold wind whistling round my ears whilst you renege on your maternal responsibilities, you have another think coming. I rest my case for tonight; I'll visit you again tomorrow if I may.

Oh no, I can hear a wailing from further down the field now – sounds like another orphan. These really are a bad lot. It is a reflection of contemporary living I suppose, decline of the family and all that. It all comes back to *bonding*.

In sheep, there are two contributory factors. First, there is all this drug-taking these days; they seem to be for ever having needles stuck in their woolly skins. It is not natural.

Secondly there is the question of all these mixed marriages. At one time, the country was 'sheeped' with breeds like Oxfords, Dorsets, Herdwicks, etc. Now, what are we instructed to do? Put the Blue-Headed Leicester on the Blackface (I can imagine a little 'consumer resistance' here) to produce the 'Mule' which is a good milk producer. Next, we put a pure-bred like a Suffolk on to the Mule to produce 'hybrid vigour' – fat lambs for market. No one *thinks* to ask the poor sheep what they think. . . . Bound to cause problems . . . with *bonding* . . . motherhood . . . life in general.

Ah well, I think that will do for tonight. I cannot hear any more distress calls, and it's getting dark.

Of course, he has not always done the lambing alone (well, alone with the resident workforce of Kevin and able members of the family). At one time we had a wonderful old shepherd who was finishing his working days on a lowland farm after a lifetime on the hill. Old Jim was a character, well known the length and breadth of the county, at all levels of society, one of a dying breed. He was equally at home in the sheep pens as in 'the best sitting room' of the farmhouse, where I can see him now, chatting up my husband-to-be's maiden aunt on the occasion of my 'meet the workers' party', or initiation ceremony, call it what you will.

The gathering was split into two rooms, the division being

one of sex, and the stiff little group, sitting on the edge of their chairs sipping Martini, were delighted and relieved at this, the highlight of the proceedings. Whether Auntie Mary was quite so thrilled was another matter. I rather feel she enjoyed the diversion, a character in her own right.

Where are all these characters in the world now? I can see Old Jim striding over the fields, his spare frame erect against the winds, with his two dogs, Bill and Jill. I can hear him calling them, his gruff voice rising in exasperation. 'Bill's blind and deaf, you know,' he would explain apologetically. It is a wonder he had any voice left at all after a lifetime of shouting, but a 'voice' he had – faltering a little when I knew him towards the end of his days – for he was known as the Singing Shepherd. He even made a television appearance on one famous occasion. . . .

At one of my first lambings I remarked that it would be wonderful if babies rose to their feet at birth just as lambs did. An expression of total horror crossed the craggy features: 'How on earth would we keep you womenfolk in the house then?' I have come to understand the meaning behind these words.

Also, in days gone by, when we had more sheep, we were in the habit of taking on students for the lambing. I dreaded this side of the season more than any other as we had to accommodate them with us in the house. We had all sorts, including female veterinary students who ate us out of house and home, and may have had high grades at 'A' level but failed miserably when it came down to practical common sense. We had one student – from the shepherd's course – who could hardly make up his mind whether to be a shepherd or a monk.

We had a Japanese student, who subsequently became the only Japanese shepherd in the world, pursued by tabloids and TV; his occupation was unusual for two reasons: firstly, there are few if any sheep in Japan; secondly, generally speaking, the Japanese work in groups. Yasuo was in constant battle with his heritage and, one morning, disappeared over the horizon, never to be seen again. I would dearly love to know what happened to him.

Yes, some of our students were easier to live with than others. One stood out, head and shoulders above the others and we soon discovered why. Brian was already a shepherd, despite his youth, but had been sent to do the year-long course at Newcastle by his employer. As there was little he did not know about sheep, you might question the wisdom of this. However, during the year, he met a little shepherdess, who subsequently became his wife and they now count sheep together. I can picture him now, standing in the shed, amid hundreds of ewes, with lambs appearing in all directions, his rather sad face expressionless. 'I don't know where they all come from,' he used to remark in a matter-of-fact way, as he tirelessly began the job of sorting out and penning up.

The pens were often subdivided, Heath Robinson style, at this, the peak of the proceedings. How did he remember which ewe belonged to which lamb and vice versa? But do it he did, calmly and patiently, talking to the woolly creatures constantly. The sight of all those faces turned towards mine as I opened the door of the shed looked to me like a nightmare for 'What's the Difference' addicts. On a brief visit shortly before they were married, his intended was heard to declare, 'I like sheep.'

You know all that work that Fred did, painting in the holiday cottage, bringing the place really up to scratch? Well, we had a couple staying for a few days, a welcome, out-of-season booking. They brought their dogs. I like people to bring dogs and children; this is a good place for dogs, with all the wide open spaces, and also we do have a sort of 'garden' in which to restrain them. I have a theory that those bringing pets or children are happier with a bit of curling wallpaper and chipped paintwork, it makes their holiday more relaxed.

Anyway, chipped paintwork is one thing, but these big dogs were left inside the house whilst 'Mummy' and 'Daddy' were out, enjoying themselves. This resulted in a little canine dissatisfaction shown in huge scratches all down the doors, and even on window sills.

What am I going to do? I would hardly say that the tourist season is about to go into full swing at this time of year, but around Easter we have a preliminary half-turn in readiness for the constant movement of the summer months. The weather is of course not reliable here at any time and certainly not in April; in fact, the only other occasion we were blocked in occurred in April. . . . The weather at the moment is mercifully mild; it makes all the difference to the mortality rate of the dear little you-know-whats in the field.

However, not only is he busy outside but she is becoming increasingly active inside. The holiday cottage is always busier than the Bee-and-Bee department. We have folk in the cottage at all times of the year, birdwatchers, ramblers and other nuts – er, I mean naturalists – or simply those wanting to get away from it all. I have made one or two refinements this year, apart from Fred's painting. I have removed the cooker with the wobbly grill door and substituted for it an auction purchase which looks better and whose doors stay closed. The only problem seems to be that you can only use one 'area' at a time. Thus, if you have a joint in the oven, you cannot boil an egg on the top – or anything else! This interesting feature was not discovered until after installation. It should prove a challenge to the enthusiastic cook; I hope that we don't have many of these.

I feel bound to repaint the doors. It looks so easy when others do it. Why is it that I end up covered with the stuff? It is in my hair, on my glasses (worn to protect the eyes), up my nose, on my clothes, shoes and splattered over everything within a radius of ten yards. Nor do the doors look all that good when I have finished them. It would have helped if I had managed to match the colour. The task is at last completed; at least it looks as if I have *tried*.

Attention is turned to more familiar ground, like sticking down wallpaper which has risen with the damp. I have a pot of wonderful stuff which serves this purpose well, even if my mother does sniff and say flour and water is what she uses; no doubt she is right, she usually is.

The bathroom is bad, the expensive spongeable vinyl paper curling uniformly at the bottom. I have a brainwave, and purchase some self-sticking, patterned border paper. I feel sure that the horizontal double row of teddies, in contrast to the blue vertical stripes of flowers does not detract from the bathroom's allure.

What next? After the spurt of winter guests, I removed all the bedding for checking, so there is that to bring back. It is an odd phenomenon, but a car filled with four duvets, two sleeping bags, ten blankets and the corresponding sheets and covers, will hold few additional items. However, my heart melts at a tear-stained face, and a couple of 'little people' manage to squash down the pile. What else is there to do?

I once had the horrific experience of being inspected by a young and enthusiastic tourist officer. I was dreading her arrival, literally trembling with fear and trepidation. I relaxed when I saw her stepping out of her car. Had she been superbly glamorous and elegant in her ensemble, I think I might have locked myself in the loo and allowed 'my better half' to do the honours; I expect a woman like that might have found him 'quaint'. No, this lady was no beauty. Fancy wearing a hairstyle like that with a nose of those dimensions! And the colour of her crimplene suit was quite wrong for her ginger hair.

I was taking in all these details whilst sitting at the kitchen table half-listening to her talking about *standards*. Slowly, it dawned on me that this lady, despite her appearance, was not one to be dallied with. We thereafter proceeded to the holiday cottage, which she inspected room by room, as if there was a rather nasty smell about two inches from her nose. It was then that I decided that something would simply have to be done about the door of the grill, but there seemed to be a positive paucity of enthusiasm amongst the electrical fraternity in these parts for such a task. Then, it was unfortunate that one of the mirrors of the dressing table would fall off if touched; it was fine if you did not touch it. Furthermore, I prayed she would not notice that the bed upstairs was missing a leg, this omission being rectified by a large block of wood. I do not know whether she did or not. She did not mention it.

Afterwards, she decided that, having made this long and arduous journey into the outback, she would have a 'quick look round the bed-and-breakfast accommodation in the farmhouse'. I did try to explain to her that this particular area was not yet fully operational, as I scurried behind her purposeful figure striding upstairs. It really was most unfortunate that, amongst the damp towels all over the bathroom floor, there was a dirty nappy.

'Oh, I see you've been re-wiring,' she exclaimed, with reference to the patches and strips of naked wall through the antiquated, peeling wallpaper. We considered it wise not to admit that this particular 'improvement' had in fact taken place a number of years previously. Nevertheless, she was quiet throughout the remainder of her inspection.

At last, she departed in her pristine white Fiesta with the doggy-gate, behind which lay her long-suffering and very clean labrador. Her face was set into almost mask-like immobility as she uttered the words, 'I'll be writing to you shortly.'

Within a few days, I was the recipient of two closely type-written foolscap sheets of specified required improvements, neatly enumerated.

Well, all that was a long time ago and I hope that if she saw us today – God forbid for I don't feel strong enough after all my hard work – she would be satisfied.

Now we come to the mass movement upwards in the farmhouse, in order to accommodate all these lovely people this coming season. On paper, this sounds quite simple. The older children rise up to the attics which are carpetless, curtainless and wallpaperless, but they don't seem to mind. Ma and Pa and the younger contingent move into the rooms vacated by the others over the kitchen, thus leaving the whole of the front of the house for the Bee and Bees.

The Bee and Bees enter the house in grandeur by means of the front door, using the dining room and 'best sitting room' (subsequently christened 'the piano room' after the purchase of a painted instrument at an auction for the princely sum of two pounds), and the bedrooms above them. They use the sweeping, wide front staircase, whilst we use the narrow, bare backstairs going up from the kitchen. In theory, they have their own toilet with wash handbasin, but every so often the cry echoes through the house, 'any bed and brekkies in?' followed by the sound of hurried footsteps upwards. The bathroom has unfortunately to be shared.

All this upheaval is very arduous. Piles of clothes (yes, piles of clothes again) are transferred from room to room and drawer to drawer, some drawers being a little too small for the offerings they are bound to receive. All this in the interests of diversification. However, there is an element of excitement amongst the children about moving – the only excitement they are likely to get – and we all await what the season has to offer this year.

We do not have to wait very long. We seem to attract a few vegetarians, one after another, this year. I welcome vegetarians, with whom I empathise, and their visits give me the opportunity to try out recipes from a beautiful book my brother sent me for my birthday. My husband will eat these dishes, but with a slightly heroic air, and if he can slip discreet references to lamb cutlets or steaks into the post-prandial conversation, he will.

We actually play host to a vegetarian family from Texas, which somehow seems a contradiction in terms. Samantha enthuses about my dishes and declares in that wonderfully rich accent – in marked contrast to her delicately ornamental appearance – that I could go straight out and open a restaurant in Texas, it would be a *wow*. Samantha is a talker and a teacher, and I am soon listening to her family history, not to mention her marital aberrations.

Then on returning to the kitchen after a visit to the washing line, a wonderful sight meets my eyes: several of my children seated at the kitchen table, obediently drawing pictures of what they like doing. The end-products are subsequently snapped neatly into her portfolio, to be taken back to show her class in the States. Quite a girl is Samantha.

She solemnly hands me a white card on departure. Close scrutiny shows that this is an invitation to a 'Womens' Day of Peace' in which she feels I might be interested. I am, but the venue (Dallas) in August, this year, leads me sadly to decline.

Now, we have another 'dietary peculiarity group', two couples with instructions which read 'no red meat or exotic fish'. What have we now, I ask myself? I cannot wait. . . . Well, at first glance there does not seem any obvious abnormality. One pair thin, and the other pair not so thin. Mr and Mrs Thin have a dog and sympathise with the lot of their furry and less fortunate friends, hence their aversion to red meat (factory farming). On questioning carefully, it is apparent that their sympathy does not stretch to birds, possibly a touch of the chickens-are-stupid-creatures-deserve-to-be-kept-in-cages philosophy. Also, it is no good my rubbing my hands contemplating continental breakfasts all round: bacon and sausages are OK apparently.

Never mind, they are harmless, if humourless, and the dog is personalised to the point of being forced to wipe its feet prior to all entrances – I like it. At the end of their surprisingly smooth stay I check to see if the answers to my guess-the-occupation game were right. Oh dear, I haven't done very well on this one. Mr Thin, whom I had thought to be a post office worker or librarian, turns out to be a customs and excise officer. Mr Fat, whom I had labelled as a transport manager, turns out to be a teacher (and I have always prided myself on my ability at detecting teachers).

Now, the ladies are rather exciting. Unlike some guests, I have had little conversation with them during their four-day stay and can only make educated guesses based on appearance. My mouth drops open about six feet and I can hardly prevent myself from falling to my knees in admiration when Mrs Thin, whom I had dismissed as a book-keeper/clerk, turns out to be a horse trainer.

Mrs Fat, a little more predictably, is a hospital catering officer. Having been on the receiving end more than once I rather wish she were not leaving as I would like to discuss this question at some length; perhaps it is just as well. To my astonishment, both she and Mr Thin compliment me on my meals (despite the odd omissions) and they all depart contented. What more can I ask?

Next, we have Stephanie the sailor's wife, who has been coming for years. On this occasion in fact, she is minus her spouse, who is off Japan or is it Mexico? However, she brings her daughters, mother, brother and friend, a nice self-contained little house-party. We do get such multiples from time to time, who make their own entertainment, demand very little and, what is more, tidy up after themselves. This is good.

Stephanie's elder daughter takes on the welfare of her younger sibling and even incorporates ours. I can see the usually scruffy, egg-encrusted faces, lined up in the bathroom, meekly being subjected to Alice's non-too-gentle ministrations with a face cloth. This really is all good stuff, not only a house full of perfect guests but also the sub-contracting out of maternal duties. They are enjoying themselves. Raucous laughter from the dining room echoes round the house well into the night, perhaps related to that outsize bottle of wine surreptitiously smuggled in or, as I like to think, attributable to our relaxed atmosphere and good food.

'. . . and we'll be back in the summer when Sean is home,' Stephanie announces happily on their departure.

'Give him a good going over first,' we joke. 'We don't want any strange diseases.' On one famous occasion, he came out in spots during his stay and set off a trail of chickenpox victims all over the county. Stephanie giggles obligingly. It is so nice for my husband to have someone to laugh at his jokes.

No sooner have they gone than we have a rash of Australians. It is apparently the season for such sorties, the cheapest time of year for our friends from down under to visit us up over. We meet some charming colonials but they share certain characteristics and habits, apart from exhibiting a dehydrated epidermis.

No, none of them requires evening meal. Instead, they carry huge insulated bags up to their rooms, filled with food – but, more importantly, bottles. We are not talking about the odd measures of hard stuff here, or cans of beer to quench the thirst. I have seen a range that any self-respecting cocktail cabinet would be proud to display, lemon slices and all, and one lot which has obviously been doing the Grand Tour, sports a bottle of ouzo in their bag. The food to accompany such exotic beverages is simple – crisps, pies, etc. As with all foreign visitors, we are the Holy Island stop, the one between York and Edinburgh. People are predictable.

It is 12.20 am and needless to say the farmer and his lady are fast asleep, even though the former has not been abed long. It is slightly disquieting, therefore, to hear a banging on the bedroom door which is obviously not one of the children who would simply barge straight in. We try to ignore it for a moment or two, perhaps it is the wind.

'James!'

We recognise the voice of a regular Bee and Bee breaking the silence, and the object of his address wriggles reluctantly out from the pillow under which his head is lying.

'Yes?' he ventures weakly at last.

'We've got a lamb downstairs. It seems to have lost its mother and it is cold.'

'Lost? Cold?'

Wearily, he crawls out of bed and pulls on his dressing gown. You know, if he is going to make appearances like this often, he really ought to have another. The old tweed creation which hardly closes and exposes vast areas of hairy leg simply will not do. Impervious to such sartorial details, he leaves his wife wondering for a moment or two before she drifts off into blissful oblivion once more. Some time later she is awakened with determination by grim, loud muttering, impossible to ignore.

'There she sits in front of the fire cradling the bloody thing in her arms . . . singing to it. . . .'

'Er what, dear?'

'The lamb of course. The lamb they found lost outside. It must have escaped somehow from the field. Great big strapping, healthy creature!'

'I hope it didn't do anything in the sitting room!'

'I was hoping it had done something on her dress . . . no, it hadn't.'

'What have you done with it?'

'Put it in a box.'

Need I ask? Next morning, the healthy infant has overturned its temporary accommodation beside the oven and crapped all over the kitchen floor.

Another aspect of lambing which can be tedious is the slow process of moving out mums and babes to the field proper, often far away, where they are to spend the summer. In order to reach the land of milk and honey, many obstacles have to be surmounted and the journey is a long one. It is here that having a large family can be advantageous.

Here we are then! Picture the scene. It is a perfect spring morning when mummy and daddy decide to go on a nice walk with their little ones – plus about ninety sheep. Once out of the field, the object is to move them down the lane to the path leading to the field. It is really not far, perhaps a mile altogether, and on paper looks quite a simple and pleasant procedure. Everything does – on paper. One thing which strikes you as you assemble in the lane is the level of noise. Who says living in the country is peaceful? There are about thirty fond mothers calling their babes to their sides, and about sixty dear little woolly creatures all wriggling round squeaking and escaping in all directions; some into the hedge, some back to the field on the other side. A child is detailed to crawl through the middle of the hedge, another instructed to walk down through the field on the other side.

We're off, a human 'pusher' encouraging the flow forward with the tip of a boot from time to time. It is soon obvious to the participant that it is not the straightforward manoeuvre imagined by townsfolk and storybook readers. One-step-forward-two-back must be an expression coined from such an experience.

Hello, what is going on here?

One very irate lady suddenly appears from the front line and purposefully and speedily advances towards an innocent six-year old who has never liked animals anyway and from this day forward is unlikely to change his opinion. Not content with knocking him to the ground with the full weight of her woolly body behind her horned head, she proceeds to stand on his back in the triumph of the victor, stamping one foot rather than waving a clenched fist. A most extraordinary spectacle and quite unfair: he only came along because he had to, hanging back to the rear in a little dreamworld of his own – unlike some of the others, who could have been accused of using methods of persuasion not recommended by the RSPCA. Needless to say, he is more than a little distressed by the incident, and his mother rushes forward and administers swift retribution to the departing ewe with the full force of her welly boot before scooping up a sobbing and none-too-clean child.

'You're all right!' How often do I say that? The words of comfort cover all contingencies from urticaria to appendicitis.

On we go, a little more cautiously this time. Here she comes again without warning, but this time the object of her animosity manages to escape through barbed wire at a speed far exceeding his personal best. We are all on our toes now. She even threatens the farmer, much to the delight of the boys. Before we reach the end of the lane we can all recognise the horned head, wild eyes and generally unkempt appearance of this fiercely protective mother – perhaps these are the symptoms of a vitamin or mineral deficiency. Surely she'll settle down after a few days in the field?

I think, generally speaking, it is safer in the garden where I am really trying hard and have at last dug over the vegetable patch. I know I haven't done it properly, but it will do. Now we come to the more exciting part, planting the tatties or spuds as we used to call them down south. They have been lying around in the dairy in the prescribed manner and to my astonishment, in the sudden moist, mild spell, have grown all manner of long limbs. Never mind, I expect they will be all right. I seem to be getting on well. I whistle as I work – well, hum. I look round after a while.

'What on earth are you doing?'

My inevitable follower is 'helping'.

'Look what I've found, Mum!'

Oh no – he is obligingly lifting out the tubers almost as fast as I am planting them. I try to be patient and understanding, it must be difficult for the poor dears to recognise the two distinct processes of planting and harvesting.

'Why the hell don't you go and help Daddy,' I scream.

Once I have finally completed this job, I grub out the raspberries and tie them with baler twine. Quite professional this looks. Now for the strawberry patch – are there any strawberry plants beneath all these weeds? Every year it is the same. I sort them out with the aim of keeping them tidy with a hoe all season, whereas I usually end up uncovering them twice a year, hopefully harvesting succulent red berries in between.

Hello, someone else joins us. A Blackface mother has come through the fence from the garden field. She is quite certain that the grass is greener here, and she is right as the lawn mower has not operated so far this year. But then, the operator has more important things to do.

Two of the children demand their own 'patch' and sow their seeds with excitement, bypassing the instructions on the packet about raking to a fine tilth and sowing thinly, and hurling the contents in one fell swoop.

'Pooh! Are you going somewhere, Mummy?'

'Where did you get that thing round your neck, Mummy?'

'Why are you wearing a skirt?'

'What are those things on your legs?'

Yes, I must admit that evening excursions are rare and just now I wish that they were even more rare. The venue? The Local WI where I am to give a talk on 'The Joys of being a Farmer's Wife.'

Here I stand then, trembling before a sea of faces expectantly raised towards mine. There seem to be hundreds, well, at least fifteen. The secretary (our landlord's wife) smiles encouragingly. It is just as well she does, this is supposed to be a humorous talk and smiles let alone laughs, are in short supply. Despite frequent rehearsal, I decide that staring at my notes is preferable to eye contact. It crosses my mind that perhaps by some sort of freak of nature, I have lapsed into Urdu or Swahili, because my words are being received in the total silence of non-comprehension.

I soldier on bravely. I have been working on this monologue for days and have been assured by my nearest and dearest that it is brilliant. I do try not to rush. How many more pages until I can slink away back to anonymity?

At last I reach the end. There is a short pause after which the president instructs the audience to 'show their appreciation in the usual manner', which they obediently do. Oh no – never again!

Then, I have to remain 'in situ' whilst they conduct their affairs, thinking only of escape. But no, I now have to judge the ginger snaps – a reasonably easy task as only one exhibit looks and tastes like anything resembling the biscuit. Luckily, I have chosen the right one.

Can I go now? No, I have to stay for supper at the table

of the president, secretary and another dignitary. Tea? Yes please (in the absence of anything stronger). I sit in silence, painfully aware of my fiasco, trying to blend in with the chair and hoping that my presence will go unnoticed. There is only one crumb of comfort on my plate: at least I shall never be asked to do such a deed again.

It is egg delivery day again and I am sitting in the beautifully decorated and furnished sitting room of Mr and Mrs Smith's bungalow, which they have only inhabited a short time. I nervously perch on the edge of my chair, wondering where 'they' have gone.

'Don't worry. They are all right.'

How often have I heard these words! People just do not realise the heights the imaginative and inquisitive child will reach. In order to convey the type of crime likely to be committed, I give a summary of recent antics at the farm of my brother-in-law. I am told that when he was in the charge of his father, he first changed the programme on the washing machine, proceeded to overturn a rather nice planted bowl, and then changed the message on the Ansaphone. He crowned his afternoon's activities by de-activating the CB radio. Mrs Smith digests this information for a few moments (she is a very fond grandmother). Then, she closes her eyes. 'How wonderful!' she breathes. I relax.

At my next port of call I am informed that my husband has been trying to track me down, for reasons unspecified. I try to phone him, unsuccessfully – the emergency must have been overshadowed by a sheep. When I arrive home, I am greeted with the news that the younger school boys have head lice and have come home with the advice to purchase the necessary treatment from the nearest chemist as soon as possible.

Thus, the car reverses out the way it came in, leaving me with a number of itchy-headed children and the prospect of a busy evening ahead! To while away the time, they line up like monkeys in a great game of counting nits in each other's hair. What a ritual follows when he returns with the cure. Worse than sheep dip it really is.

On another trip, I drop one child off at a party in the village. It is easy to find the house of a children's party, invariably the one where the father is to be seen earnestly pottering in the greenhouse, head well down. I drop the child and he is immediately joined from nowhere by what looks like dozens of clones. Some fathers, of course, do not have to invent chores in the greenhouse, especially at this time of year. They can just slope off to the lambing shed when the going gets tough and spend a quiet afternoon ringing lambs. . . .

The doctor is an important figure in our life, a toss-up whether we see more of him or the vet. They both play golf on the nearby golf course, incidentally. Today we are going to visit the doctor and we are sitting in the luxuriously carpeted waiting room of the spanking new surgery. We actually rather enjoy these outings, unless someone is seriously ill, of course. There are copies of glossy magazines to read, the seats are softly upholstered, it is gloriously warm, the children play happily in the house, with all the toys. Such a pity that someone must have decided that the waiting patient should be soothed by the strains of suitable music from which there is no escape. At last we are summoned over the intercom to the inner sanctum. Nothing serious today, just a rash resistant to treatment.

'We have a pet lamb in our garage,' he announces surprisingly. One of his farming friends has asked him to look after it as it has a broken leg. 'It's a lovely little thing. Perhaps you'd like to pop in and have a look at it?'

71

May

As we move slowly out of the post-lambing period, the farmer's fancy turns to thoughts of *cows*, which have not hitherto been headline news so far as the farmer's wife is concerned. What this means is that they have quietly been getting on with the job in hand, being bother to no one. It is vaguely irritating to be on the receiving end of various pieces of bovine advice during pregnancy and lactation – I don't suppose I am alone in having suffered from this – and you gradually come to the conclusion that, if cows can do it, you can, within certain specified limitations of course. Since the domestic cow is pregnant and lactating continuously for most of her life and does not complain – why should you? Anyway, I really have to admit a certain fondness for the cow.

Mind you, we have had our 'rough patches' with cows, and their obstetric histories have not always been trouble-free. There was another May many years ago when for cow after cow we had to call the vet, the result being major surgery in every case. We had twenty-one Caesars in all that spring – the stage was reached where the assistants knew the procedure almost as well as the experts. By the time the vet arrived – and frequently a rather frail-looking lady performed the operation alone – the cow would be 'prepped' (tied up in a nice clean stall), the lighting arranged strategically, soap, water and towel at the ready. Each operation had its own individual characteristics, one being memorable by a piece of gut ballooning out of the incision intermittently (which we assistants had to stuff back in); a young bystander was heard to declare that she would never eat bubble gum again. By the time we reached the last delivery by this method, the gentleman responsible for implanting such odd-shaped offspring was well on his way to meat pies.

This year I have noticed one or two cases of pronounced postnatal depression in the herd, even if the actual act of parturition has not been too painful. I expect that the psychologists would say that if sufficient struggle has not occurred, then an opposing reaction is bound to set in some time later. Funny how psychologists are rarely women.

One of our ladies was exceptional in arranging her own therapy after the traumatic delivery of a product that was to be honest, enormous – it made my eyes water in sympathy. This poor matron spies the large cool lake in the next field and fancies a dip. Off she waddles with slow movement. Aaaah, yes, the effort was worth it. She lies in the therapeutic waters luxuriously.

Once she feels she has had sufficient aquatic therapy for one session, she tries to climb out of the pond, with no success. Then she tries again, and again, her infant regarding the spectacle from the safety of dry land in wonder. She finally falls back into the water exhausted, and waits for help. Here he comes; I would not exactly call him a knight in shining armour, but damsel in distress she certainly is. And reinforcements are on the way in the person of Kevin on tractor, complete with ropes and ladders.

At last, the cow is out. The calf is pleased and the rescuers are pleased, if a little damp. The chief protagonist in this drama, however, remains unmoved, mentally. Blow me if, next morning, the sight from the bathroom window doesn't reveal that she has done it again.

Generally speaking, I do feel that cows have more character than sheep. *And* due to the fact that there are fewer of them, even I can recognise one or two, usually the Jersey-cross, because she has such lovely eyes and long eye lashes, or the Romanola-cross because of her oddly patterned coat. He can recognise each and every one of course, and can trot out their breeding line like the course commentator at Epsom. 'Just like her mother,' she is heard to mutter, as a particular lady delivers a smart blow with her back leg as he endeavours to inspect a new addition and, let's face it – what a compliment to be described as a 'good milker'. . . .

'Now, the euphoria of the immediate postnatal period is soon dispelled if one looks down and to one's surprise, sees two heads suckling instead of one. One head is certainly mine but this other – well, it bears no resemblance to my family at all; I'll just give it a kick – that should do the trick. Oh no, he has certainly gone away but then so has my Cedric. Here they are, both back again. I'll give him another kick. The same thing happens, somehow they seem to be joined. If I let Cedric suck, I have to let this new fellow in too. Extraordinary!'

Yes, the twinning harness is a great affair, any animals who fall into the category of being 'good milkers' (I am surprised he has never suggested strapping an extra one on to his wife) being often subjected to this treatment.

'Well, it's profitable. I just pop up the road to the dairy and purchase a calf, hitch it on for a day or two and Bob's your uncle – she'll soon take the two. Then, when it comes to selling time, I get the price of two instead of one. It's economics. You've got to have your head screwed on in this game I tell you. . . .'

Watching the unfortunate infants trying to refresh themselves, it looks as if they could do with having their heads screwed on a little less tightly.

'Yes, we've got the poor old soul sorted out this year, haven't we, dears?'

'You mean that, because Ferdinand seemed to lose his libido last summer we should be able to keep the boss on his toes well into the autumn? Ha ha.'

'I feel quite sorry that I have already delivered, with no fuss or carry on either. Mind you, I suppose it was only fair after last year.'

'What happened last year?'

'Why you remember! No, I don't suppose you do. You've a

*head like a sieve. It's because you had your horns removed,
a mistake I reckon, not natural!'*

*'But, my dear, everyone has their horns removed these
days.'*

*'Well, I am hanging on to mine. Anyway, what was I
saying? Oh yes, last year, I had a breech. Had to be brought
in, you know. It is pretty uncomfortable trotting along with
a couple of feet poking out of your rear end I can tell you.
Anyway, they finally got me into the emergency cubicle and
tied the ropes to my poor Herbert's feet and pulled – it was
absolutely excruciating – but still nothing happened.*

'It must have been awful for you.'

*'Well, I was very brave. Didn't make too much noise. Of
course, in the end, they had to call out that twit of a vet. He
had some fancy gadget, I don't know what it was called. I
managed to shower him with you-know-what in the process.
I might have laughed if it hadn't been quite so painful. You
should have seen his face – all over his moustache! Anyway,
it did the trick.*

*'Herbert was touch-and-go for a day or two and I might
tell you I didn't feel too clever myself. And, do you know, I
never felt Herbert was – well – normal. I wonder if his brain
might have been affected – lack of oxygen or something. He
was always a difficult child; very slow to feed at first, then,
couldn't get enough. I was skin and bone – that bad summer
too – and he simply never did what he was told. He was
always wandering off. I don't mind telling you, I was glad to
see the back of him. I know it's an awful thing to say about
your own flesh and blood but. . . . Anyway, I hope Daisy is
easier. . . .'*

'Girls often are.'

*'Do you think so, I'm not too sure about that. I remem-
ber. . . .'*

There is nothing like a good moo.

We have had the Aga off and back on again about three
times. 'I wish you'd make up your mind.' Well, May is a

tricky month, and it has been such a funny year after that cold spell.

I loathe winter but I do love my Aga, especially when I come down on a dark and chilly morning, wishing I had been able to stay buried beneath the blankets. Some of our friends take it in turns as to who should get up first, in some cases, the husband always gets up first. 'Some of us' call this sort of behaviour effeminate – is it effeminate to crawl shivering down the stairs, dragging behind you reluctant school children with whom you know you are going to be battling for the next half-hour? On such mornings, the warming presence of the Aga calms and comforts.

It is as well that I have some support from some source, in the absence of 'anyone else'. Yes, not only do we cook on the Aga but chilly bodies dress beside it and warm their socks on it. Therefore, much as I welcome the light, warmer mornings of May, it is with great sadness that I finally turn the switch.

Now, I am at the mercy of that temperamental monstrosity in the scullery. It is such a paradox that at the time of year I am most pressed on the cooking front, I have to resort to this inefficient creature, otherwise I have a constant supply of heat at varying temperatures at the ready. C'est la vie! No one wants to visit Northumberland in midwinter and who can blame them? The transition is tricky: I forget to put the oven on; then, I forget to turn it off. I boil pans over. . . .

Yes, the weather is warming up nicely. Even the horse yawns as I dismount after a less invigorating hour than usual. Flies! We have hardly rid ourselves of our winter visitors, many of whom simply stay the year round anyway (life is just too easy for some), when *zoom* in come the summer ones. However, a few sprays with that foul-smelling stuff and the flies are dead. Mind you, I don't know how any self-respecting winged insect dares to enter the premises where he might be attacked by a number of small boys, armed with a variety of weapons. It is certainly the best use I've seen for that book of '500 What's What Jokes'. Right, that will do for now, folks. I know it is good fun but it is *flies* you are supposed to be hitting. It is rapidly turning into a free-for-all.

There are 'things' in the garden too. I am derided for pouring bucket after bucket of soapy water over my beloved lupins morning and night. I sometimes think I overdo it. Any horticultural expert entering the garden after such an outpouring might feel he was having a bad dream, parts of plants appearing to be covered with a weird fungus – either that or it is the Year of the Cuckoo Spit. I have tried everything on these aphids, both chemical and kind, and nothing seems to work. I discuss the problem with Bert, when I meet him in the queue at the Co-op.

'You want to plant those what-do-you-call-its. You know, them things what like dry weather.'

'Cacti?'

Bert carries on regardless as usual, delving into his vast fund of useful information.

'French marigolds. They attract summat what likes aphids.'

'Oh.'

The problem is, where am I going to put them? I have planted my sweet peas, the self-supporting kind, with which I have had some success in previous years. I have also planted asters in abundance at the front of the 'rose bed', interspersed with stocks and other odd unconventional mixtures. Mind you, from where I am standing at the moment, there seems little chance of this region ever bursting into the anticipated riot of bloom, colour and texture.

Actually, I sometimes wonder why I bother. I sowed my courgettes on the kitchen windowsill, then soon discovered that 'something' was eating the seeds – yes, another mouse crime. I had wondered why so many of my sweet peas had failed to germinate but by this time it was too late to sow more. I have sown more courgettes, though – and 'hidden' the trays in the safety of the office. Apart from the lack of rain and surfeit of insects and other pests, we frequently suffer assaults from marauding chickens, not to mention footballs and pairs of clumsy feet behind. It really is a wonder anything grows at all.

The rhubarb patch is reminiscent of 'The Day of the Triffids', but I feel an enormous sense of achievement when I actually pull some, about ten tons of it. What on earth I am going to do with it is anyone's guess, though there have been one or two suggestions as it is not the most popular fruit in this house. I stagger indoors, laden, buckling at the knees. Hours later, I stand exhausted but satisfied, surveying my many sparkling jars of rhubarb and ginger jam. No one likes that either.

Perhaps I will weed the strawberry patch again, even if the weeds are not growing so fast this year. Yes, that's one thing about a dry garden, even the weeds cannot help but be discouraged a little by the lack of refreshment. This time, I have the dubious assistance of Number Two Son. Unfortunately, he never stops talking, topics ranging from who plays left-half for Everton to the full, comprehensive list of his dietary preferences (as if I didn't know). If all this were not wearing enough, I turn round halfway through the task to find that the 'weeds' he is busy flinging into the barrow with such abandon are strawberry flowers. Another poor crop ahead!

I am now at a garden centre. If farming is on the decline, with many going bust, the rest just managing to scrape a living from rock-bottom prices – the garden industry is blossoming. In recent years several local garden centres have sprung up on what was barren before. And fascinating places they are too.

'What can you grow in a garden whose sandy soil is dry as a bone, and is beset by gales, greenfly, hens and small boys?'

The assistant's smile seems fixed. She does not give up; she stands firm.

'. . . that is colourful, does not require dead-heading and *spreads*. . . .'

The breath seems to go out of her in an enormous sigh.

'Have you tried grass?' she answers wearily at last.

It does not matter. I get carried away just the same. I wander around, scooping up a box of this, a box of that. . . . I'll put these in the front border now the daffodils are dying down, brighten up the front of the house to cheer the arriving Bee and Bees. Box after box is piled into the car.

'Where are *we* going to sit?' they wail.

This is the time of year when I take on a little part-time job. After the older children come home from school he is quite happy to sit with them and the papers as the pressures of the last weeks finally ease off. I eagerly set off on foot for an hour or so, glad of the escape. The workplace is unusual, a large area of uneven ground, its far boundary being the stream where we often see heron or swan – even a kingfisher one spring. The present incumbents are of course sheep, and it is my job to see that there are none in the ignominious position of being stuck on their backs, unable to regain their feet because of their heavy pre-clipping coats. Simple soul that I am, I always feel so thrilled when I actually find such an unfortunate – rectifying the animals' predicament is one of the rare feats I can perform unaided. Oh, what happened to that efficient secretary/PA bristling with ideas and responsibilities of long, long ago?

As a matter of fact, I often dash towards creatures who are merely resting, rather alarming for the poor lady in question to see this wild-eyed, unkempt woman advancing towards her with great speed and a good deal of 'there, there, dears' and 'don't worry, you'll soon be all right.' The terrified soul rises with unprecedented alacrity and gallops off with great speed to the far corner of the field.

As instructed, I walk round the outside of the field, close to the stream, not that I would be of much use if there were a case of 'swimmer in difficulties'. I can hardly swim myself and mouth-to-mouth resuscitation with a sheep is not my idea of a joke. It does not matter how often I tread this path, the sudden sight of swans as they round the bend never fails

79

to cause a sharp intake of breath. They are so big, so beautiful, so regal. There is something awesomely alarming in the rearing of that elegant long white neck and the slight rising of the wings; the soft hiss compounds the necessity for caution. Don't worry, dear, I wouldn't dream of coming any closer.

The swans nest every year in this stream, as do the striking black-and-white shelduck who make their home in rabbit holes in the hillocks of the saltgrasses.

Today is special. I feel it the minute I enter the field. What is that movement over there? There is another . . . and another. . . . I am wearing my specs so I should be able to see. I remove, polish on my hanky and replace. Yes, sure enough, the hillock I am very slowly approaching is the home of a family of fox cubs.

I stand spellbound, really close now, able to discern their pointed ears, mischievous, attractive little faces alert and looking at me. After a while, they decide here is not a force to be reckoned with and go back to playing with each other, boxing, gambolling and laughing in the sunshine of early evening. Oh, oh here is mama, tense and watchful (she looks a bit run down – I'll bet she hasn't been taking her vitamins). A word in the ear of each cub about not talking to strangers, and one by one they disappear down what seems to be individual entrances to their lovely home.

What a delightful scene, I really feel that magical sense of privilege to have witnessed it. I can hardly tear myself away; I want to wait for more, but on the other hand, I can hardly contain myself before breaking the news. I am quite confident I have a story with an 'exclusive tag' here. So often, when I report what I consider to be an exciting find, I receive a reply from the depths of the sports page, along the lines that he has been an observer for days.

When it comes to foxes, we cannot help but sit on the fence. Cubs or no cubs (all young are pretty) you cannot help but admire the beauty of line and movement of this animal in close-up or simply in a flash of colour in the distance. I admire the way he lives on his wits, frequently sharpened against those of his neighbour, the farmer; his is often a lonely life and he can run for days in fear of its ending sooner than he would like.

The admiration tends to diminish when half the hen population disappears in a cloud of feathers. It vanishes totally when a newborn lamb is taken (those which escape the net of inside deliveries). On one horrific occasion, a certain member of the fox family came upon a ewe stuck on her back in the field. Instead of pulling her to her feet again as you or I would have done, feeling a bit peckish, he helped himself to one of them. The poor creature was left in mortal agony for hours before discovery. I know we all have to live but such an incident highlights the cruel indiscrimination of his diet.

As I walk back from the field, the sight of the housemartins building their house at the corners of the windows of ours is a happy one. They too come every year. How glad we are to see them come, how sorry to see them leave in the autumn.

'What are you doing today, dear?'
   'Feet and bottoms.'
   'Oh, er, nice! Never a dull moment, eh?'
I think, by and large, generally speaking, taking a broad view of things, I would prefer to wash the floors on my hands and knees – as I am doing – as I do frequently. I don't think it does my knees much good but I like to think it is good for the waistline. It is certainly good for the soul. . . .

Later: 'I don't know, I spend all day cleaning bottoms only to come in to find another two to do.'

Yes, the younger members of the family seem to be currently afflicted with a disease affecting their lower alimentary tract.

'Come in, darling.'
   'Oh, do you think I should. . . . I mean – they've had this bug and I wouldn't want yours to get it too. . . .'
   'Balderdash, dear. They've had it! Shit from one end of the house to the other . . . blessed nuisance . . . could have

done with one of those gadgets they put on the front of the tractor . . . you know?'

'Eh, do you mean a buckrake or a snow plough?'

'Never mind. Then I had to use simply *gallons* of Dettol to get rid of the smell. What's that? Oh yes, they're all right now. Do come in for a cup of coffee. Sit down.'

'Oh, thank you. Where shall I – er – sit?'

The beautifully fitted kitchen, which always strikes me as a cross between an operating theatre and a film set, looks as if a herd of pedigree heifers have ploughed through it – or perhaps a tractor complete with buckrake and plough. There are glasses, dishes, plates, cups everywhere. They lie higgledy piggledy in heaps all over the normally gleaming work surfaces. There seems to be the entire range of French cast-iron casseroles in a bright shade of orange – with brown-encrusted interiors – jostling for position round the sinks. The floor is covered by cardboard boxes, the corrugated interiors of which are in the process of being joyfully removed by Dylan and Orlando, speedily joined by two others from my car.

'Er – have you had a party, Gwendoline?' I have just noticed that she seems to be wearing a nightdress rather than one of her usual creations – difficult to tell sometimes. Her enviable dark tresses tumble over her shoulders, and I cannot help noticing that her complexion is a little less radiant than usual. However, she still looks better than I do on a good day. I nudge some of the debris on the draining board aside cautiously and put down the eggs.

'Can I *do* something, Gwendoline?'

'Goodness me, no, darling. Mrs T. will do it; she'll be here in a minute. We had a bit of a do last night . . . just a few chums, you know. . . .'

Looks as if there were about two hundred. Poor old Mrs T. I nervously remove a tray of glasses which were balancing on a stool, set them in the sink and perch there rather uncomfortably whilst Gwendoline searches for a kettle.

'Where can it be? It must be here somewhere. . . .'

A decision is suddenly taken.

'Don't worry. I have to get back anyway.'

Hastily I retrieve my offspring from under the table, make good my escape and reflect that I am glad I live a simple life.

Things could not be more different at my next stop. There, the kitchen is fitted out like those in the 'glossies' too but here a sense of order prevails. All work surfaces are covered with rows of tempting bowls of assorted salads sparkling, dishes of fruit, flans, meringues . . . and the room is warm and redolent with the savoury scent of herbs and spices.

'Ah, Muriel, busy are you? It's all right. I'll not stop. No, I haven't brought the children. Pay me next time.'

I know the signs. Muriel is wearing her heavy plastic apron, depicting a variety of British potato, and an intense expression on her pleasant and attractive face. She 'does functions' in the area and very good she is at it too, in great demand. What is more, she and her staff come along afterwards and sweep everything away into cardboard boxes in her vehicle. What a pity she didn't 'do' Gwendoline's. . . .

The egg boxes are gradually disappearing in the back of the car. Just the pottery left.

'Ah. Come in.'

The voice belongs to a huge figure covered in hair, a little reminiscent of a Highland cow (without horns), also in an apron. Over the years Gareth and his wife have built up a thriving business in beautifully hand-painted pottery, examples of which are to be seen in smart places in the town – and further afield. They are friendly folk but the close proximity of so many breakable objects leads me to decline their hospitality when accompanied by ambulant children. An odd trip out with only baby in carrycot is a treat to be savoured. I deliver the eggs and depart. Time to return to base.

You would have thought that after taking in tourists all these years, I would have the entire process down to a fine art. This is not the case. I never set out with a definite plan of action; a system of sorts has evolved in time, tailored to suit the individual requirements of the client, of course. The emphasis is on the casual approach, though. If people come here expecting everything to be done for them – and someone ready to do it – they have come to the wrong place.

For example, we do not *wait*. Food is delivered to the dining room by the farmer, complete with quips, weather forecast and a beaming smile. I suspect on occasion that perhaps his work shirt and jeans covered in mud, etc., might not meet with the approval of the public health department but it's rustic and demonstrates that we are a *real working farm*. We did read in a Sunday supplement on farmhouse accommodation of a farmer who wore a different bow tie each night to serve at table – but we pronounced such behaviour affected.

The hot component of the meal, be it the bacon and eggs of breakfast or the main course of the evening nosh-up, is shot on to the hot plate in the dining room with aplomb. The remainder of the meal is (or should be) already 'in situ'. In the mornings, this comprises healthy orange juice and earthenware jars of cereal (it comes in a packet but I find the consumer warms to earthenware). Then, there is a jug of milk (semi-skimmed of course), home-made wholemeal bread (when I can be bothered), butter, marmalade and a platter of fruit.

In the evenings, the bread and fruit remain but the table is completed with salads, pudding, cheese and oatcakes, and I find a small vase of flowers is a good finishing touch. This approach seems to me to be 'folksy' enough without bordering on the 'trendy'. By means of an electric kettle, an unlimited supply of tea and coffee, as well as a limited supply of cups, saucers and teaspoons guests are encouraged to concoct their own beverages to their hearts' content.

The *door* is an all-important part of the non-waiting method. It is equipped with a 'ball' fastening so that it can be opened with a kick, or if this fails, a flick from one's hip if one's hands are full. However, this device makes the most infernal noise; I suspect that it could have been the prototype. No matter, what one does is set up the table with all the cold stuff and then close the door. We can be in the kitchen, filled with noisy children, Brian Redhead in full spate – and still hear when the guests approach the trough for breakfast. Now, after the waiter has taken in the steaming platter, he closes the door and leaves them to it.

That is the stage. Backstage, arrangements are nowhere near so well organised. In the mornings the cook frequently finds herself bombarded with additional orders if there is no school. The general feeling is that if she is standing, sweating at the cooker, it is a simple matter to do a few extra sausages or rashers of bacon – or even the odd egg. I suppose it is, but if I am not careful, meals tend to run together and last all day. They can manage perfectly well on cornflakes anyway (or Weetabix, Special K, Alpen, Rice Crispies, depending upon which child you are dealing with).

Once the meal has left the kitchen, I can straighten up (easier said than done), heave a sigh of relief, and then set about clearing up the debris – all 'artistes' work in a mess, I tell myself. Neither my mother nor Muriel the caterer would approve of this theory.

For a start, the grill is frequently set on fire, filling the kitchen with smoke, necessitating frantic squirting of spray and shutting of doors to contain the aroma. It is one thing for the tempting smell of sizzling rashers to rise up to the nostrils of the dressing guests upstairs; it is quite another for them to wonder whether to come down or call the fire brigade. There it is then: blackened grill, cooker covered in egg shells, crumbs and charred tomato skins, towers of cereal dishes containing a variety of residues. . . . By the time, this lot is sorted out – *click* goes the dining room door again; the meal is over, indicating further action on stage.

Now, when a 'party' comes to stay for a week or more, this moment is all-important for it is at this point that the size of the task ahead is revealed. Slowly, filled with dread, the dining room is approached. Firstly, hot plate turned off – good. Secondly, room heater turned off – excellent. Thirdly, all plates and dishes neatly stacked on the trolley – big sigh of relief. And just to put the icing on the cake, a cheery face round the door: 'That was a lovely breakfast/meal. Thank you very much.'

At the other end of the scale, there is the bombshell scene. The hot plate is left on, the serving dishes exhibit charred and firmly stuck remains, and the heat hits you on entrance. (Often heat is quite unnecessary even in the mornings but it adds that extra 'welcoming' touch, and they can always turn it off, can't they?) The table floats horrifyingly into your field of vision. Everything remains as it was used, dishes embellished with cornflakes and muesli surplus to requirements, plates with similar remnants of sausage and bacon and, naturally, 'bits' from the marmalade. Just to compound the picture, the sugar spoon has visited someone's coffee and brown stains adorn the hitherto pristine white linen. Blow me if the flowers haven't been knocked over. Hopefully, these folk will not stay long.

In between these two pictures are of course varying permutations. Our bêtes noirs are the we-would-be-staying-in-a-5-star-hotel-but-thought-it-would-be-quaint types. On the other hand, although life is made easier by kind, considerate and tidy guests – charm conquers all.

Yes, the season will soon be getting into gear, and there will not be many nights between the end of May and the beginning of September when we shall be able to flit naked to the loo along the landing.

Right – here we go.

'Good morning, Mr Irvine. Did you sleep well? Oh, good!'

I don't know what I'd say if someone responded in the negative to this question. 'Tough Titty?'

Usually, mercifully, people reply: 'Oh – like a log; I've never slept so well; I haven't taken a single pill since I've been here; it must be the air. . . .' There was one famous occasion when a gentleman guest was up and down all night, and as I am a light sleeper I hardly slept a wink myself, worrying about him. In the morning, his wife informed me that her husband never ate breakfast. On his descent, well into the morning, he engaged me in conversation during the course of which I felt almost overbalanced backwards by the power of alcoholic fumes. He was an utterly charming man and once I understood his 'infirmity' I ceased to worry.

Mr Irvine has slept well. He is an insignificant-looking, balding little man, bespectacled and wise, whom his wife despatches to our care at intervals to recharge his batteries. Goswick is all things to all men, we like to think. His stays are always mid-week as he is a man of the cloth. We have never seen his wife, sometimes, he comes with his friend, a fellow birdwatcher, sometimes alone. His rather sad, apologetic face reminds me rather of a spaniel or Bassett hound. Mr Irvine is a quiet guest, hardly making his presence felt in the house; he is TKC (tidy, kind and considerate) and laughs at my husband's jokes. Occasionally he makes a joke himself, which seems outrageously amusing due to his naturally quiet demeanour.

'Did you send a deposit, Mr Irvine?'

Goswick accounting system is less than perfect.

'My wife does all the arrangements. I really don't know.'

'Let's see, she seems to have sent a lot of letters.'

'That's her, never one word if three will do.'

How I would love to meet Mrs Irvine. I don't suppose I ever shall. I can picture her though: a large lady, forbidding, her iron-grey hair severely swept from her wide, smooth forehead, her spectacles accentuating the determined lines of her face. She'll not be wearing trousers (usually 'de rigueur' at Goswick) but a serviceable 'good' tweed skirt, dark green lambswool cardigan over a plain cream silk blouse with brooch at the neck. Mr Irvine will not be allowed to drive at more than thirty-five miles an hour or eat fried food. He will be exhorted to eat his 'greens' which I know he hates and will only be allowed to watch educational TV programmes; he will be abed by 9.30 pm with his cup of milky cocoa, whether he likes it or not. Mrs Irvine must realise the strain such a regime imposes upon her husband or she would not send him for his regular 'fixes' at Goswick. Mrs Irvine must be 'all right'.

Mr Irvine gets on well with the other guests, another attribute to add to his already comprehensive list. Some guests mingle and some do not, and if you have people staying who are part of the latter category, you have problems. You have to go out of your way to arrange staggered mealtimes (this sometimes occurs anyway for other reasons) which means that when you have the dietary requirements of your own family to fit in, you are at the cooker or kitchen sink from 7.30 am until well into the night, with the tricky operation of 'revising' the table in between.

What other guests are there this week? This is now what is called Spring Bank Holiday, what used to be called Whitsun. It brings 'em out in droves.

Mr and Mrs Diddlepowski live in London and regard our rustic accommodation and simple lifestyle as complete relaxation – so *we* relax. They are Polish and formerly lived in Poland, their English being heavily accented.

On their first morning, Mrs D. comes through to the kitchen and asks, 'Have you merk?'

Her son, called Marek, is playing with ours somewhere and I reply to this effect with confidence.

'No. I want a "merk" to put my coffee in.'

They have brought with them vast quantities of ground coffee, that subtle blend and roast that is our instant stuff is obviously not good enough. When I think of all the paraphernalia and performance a number of ladies of my acquaintance espouse in order to produce perfect coffee. . . . Mrs D. simply shoves a large spoon of the coarse grains into a large mug and adds boiling water, stirring and then allowing it to settle. The necessity for the mug is obvious.

The son is about ten years old, a bright, highly intelligent boy who slots easily into our family and his companionship is eagerly sought at all times.

Mr D. is 'in shipping' and Mrs D. is a lecturer at a big

business college in London. A couple of cute cookies we have here, I feel rather inadequate. Nevertheless, they are absolutely charming. They are also very precise, so we know exactly where we are with them. The boy comes into the kitchen each morning to announce their nutritional requirements and also of course their presence, making 'the door system' redundant.

Mr D. has a wonderful and very elaborate camera which he is obviously willing to demonstrate to interested parties. They take a trip to the Farne Islands: 'My wife, she is a bad sailor, I say to her, "watch the horizon and you will be all right; suddenly, the mist comes down – no horizon!" ' Yes, this meteorological phenomenon is par for the course on this coast I am afraid.

Midweek: 'I am chust going home for a day or two,' Mrs D. suddenly declares.

'Home? Down to London?' I squeak.

'Of course. I'll chust fly down.'

'Oh.' I feel more like a country bumpkin every day.

'I 'ave to, you see. My students are taking zair exams. I must be wiz zem.' It crosses my mind that a few teachers of our ken would rise in esteem if they displayed similar solicitude.

'Is it worth coming all the way back up again on Thursday?' (They go home on Saturday.)

'Oh – eet is!'

Say no more.

Most exciting news: a happy event is in the offing. Happy event you echo? Don't you have enough happy events down there? Why you have more happy events than . . .! No, this is different. The lady in question has only recently joined the band from up the road. Jack suddenly decided he no longer had accommodation for these little ladies and thus he despatched them down to us.

Hitherto, we have had a reasonably large contingent of hens who have lived more or less pacifically alongside our bantam cockerel. Since the arrival of this small group of bantam hens, this gentleman has been delighted. As a result, to our delight, one of the incomers has been found sitting upon a clutch of eggs. We have never had chickens before. The children are so excited and make a visitation every day, after school. The 'sitter' seems utterly unconcerned by the publicity. She regards them gravely and if anyone goes too close, she is not averse to delivering the odd peck or two.

June

'Where are you going, Mummy?'

Where do you think I am going at this time of night, in wellies, armed with a watering can? Yes, after a hard day, hours of sweat over stove and sink for the Bee and Bees, what does one do? Collapse into an easy chair, to be plied with a 'G and T', iced and lemoned by a loving husband? No such luck. No, one staggers outside and proceeds to perform these acts of primitive irrigation, with the uncomfortable knowledge of fighting a losing battle.

Talk about flaming June. This one is not just flaming, it seems to have burned off all the plant life in my garden. (I am reliably informed that the crops are OK for some reason; what I do know is that this low-lying land fares badly in wet weather so I can only conclude that the converse is true.) My garden must be composed of different stuff altogether, I don't know why. In the wet weather of last summer, it resembled a jungle; this year it is a desert. My poor little plants. . . .

I encounter Bert outside the Post Office. He says there's a lot of 'What-d'you-call-its' in the garden at the moment and they go for the fragile roots of bedding plants. Although I am sure it is kindly meant, this information gives me little comfort. I paid good money for these plants. 'You *will* grow' I mutter as I shower them from the watering can once more. The lawn is fading to a dull puce, it is the same on the nearby golf course. The assistant at the little supermarket, who is a golfing enthusiast, declares it is like playing on the moon. She is obviously better travelled than I would have credited.

So much for the flower department; the fruit and veg

section does not look too promising either. The raspberries might yield a modest quantity of ruby fruit. The strawberry patch looks very sorry for itself and in previous years what I have lacked in quantity or quality I have more than compensated by the amazingly early harvest of this fruit; perhaps someone should have activated the sprinkler? The potatoes do not look too bad, and in fact this vegetable is already gracing our table, straight from the garden.

OK so that's potatoes, but what about my peas, beans, lettuce, courgettes . . .? These do not look too clever at the moment, not too clever at all. At least, there are no slugs in the lettuces, puny offerings that they are. Bert says that's what gardening is all about, what suits one pest does not suit another. Sometimes Bert's philosophy irritates. And *that*'s another thing, you return to the house from the garden's evening ablutions scratching – and continue to scratch all night.

'Look, this is not the time to start silly games!'

'It is not a silly game. I've just invented it. It's called "Narnia!" ' There is a limit to the number of children capable of being contained in a wardrobe, especially those of the size considered suitable for the holiday cottage. On the other hand, if it keeps them amused and fairly quiet. . . .

'Have a nice weekend!' people politely exhort. People like shop assistants or hairdressers. Nice weekend! They do not seem to realise that weekends, or Bank Holidays, mean little to a farming family. True, you are relieved of the task of packed lunch preparation and can sometimes lie in bed till 7.30 am, if the younger members of the family allow. On the other hand, there are uniforms and sports kits to sort out and wash, more mouths to feed and, on most Saturdays from Easter until October, there is the vexed question of the holiday cottage (the exception being the wonderful event known as a 'fortnight's booking').

Here I am then. The minute I open the door I can forecast the magnitude of the task ahead. How? Smell! One long sniff, sometimes this is not necessary, tells all. If the only scent to reach the nostrils is a subtle blend of loo cleaner with perhaps just a hint of Ajax (a damp squeezy mop against the wall compounds the picture) I can relax, all will be well, there will be little more than a change of sheets.

On the other hand, today the mingling odours of recent and less recent cooking meet the senses, items on the menu ranging from burnt toast to kippers. Add a trace of wet dog, a dollop of damp anorak in a base of equal parts alcohol and tobacco – and you are in trouble. I take a deep breath (without sniffing) and bravely advance into the interior to inspect the damage more closely. Start upstairs, noting hairy stair carpet in the passing, and look under the beds: no sweeping or hoovering performed here.

The woodburning stove is packed full of half-combusted debris. The loo looks dubious; the bath is dirty and the bathroom floor, grey (it should be blue). The dining-room carpet seems covered in dog hair, cornflakes and other less attractive items of recent diet. I have left looking at the kitchen till last. I know what I will find there, and with sinking heart face the blackened cooker, the brown sink and the grey encrusted fridge.

Briskly, I fling open windows wide and flick on the immersion heater. There is nothing here that plenty of hot water, Fairy Liquid and elbow grease cannot cure! Oh no, the immersion heater fails to light up. Perhaps it's just a bulb or something? No, time confirms a more serious diagnosis. Dash back to base and phone our tame electrician, Ernie. Meanwhile, I continue to fill the electric kettle again and again, and attack the cottage with a ferocity which quite frightens the younger contingent coming out of the woodwork. Eventually, Ernie arrives looking pale.

'Haven't been well.'

'I am sorry to hear that, Ernie.'

Ernie is never well. In winter it is viruses, in summer it is hay fever. At the moment I suspect that it is a combination of the two.

'Yes, been off work for a week, dizzy spells too. Felt funny. Not right yet.'

He sniffs. Ernie sniffs a lot. I think perhaps it could be adenoids. He pushes a greasy lock of hair back from his eyes, reaches in his pocket for his handkerchief and blows his nose fiercely. It will probably be the most energetic act he will perform today.

'Er, it is the immersion heater, Ernie,' I begin anxiously. 'Can you fix it?' Ernie regards the contents of his handkerchief with interest, then replaces it in his pocket, from where he produces his screwdriver. Ah, this looks more promising.

'Well, I'll leave you to it, Ernie. I'll just get on with the rest of the place if you don't mind . . . time ticks by you know!' I add encouragingly.

'Come out of the wardrobe, you lot!' I shout upstairs. Ernie gives me a funny look.

'Play outside. It is a lovely day.'

It never fails to impress me that when it is raining, cold, foggy or snowing the big outdoors beckons, but when the skies are cloudless, they always opt to stay inside.

'What can we do outside?'

A few minutes later, a chance glance through the window reveals two small figures balancing on top of the high wall surrounding the building. A younger family member, whose chubby legs will not stretch so far upwards, watches them wistfully before she returns to play the game of plaguing mother, as a second choice.

'Don't you *dare* step on this floor. I've just washed it.' It is more like making mud pies actually, goodness knows what they've been doing. As for the dogs' hair, it coats the carpets so thickly that it conceals the pattern and original colour; it is way beyond the powers of the hoover, definitely another hands-and-knees job. At last I straighten my back wearily and return to the kitchen in trepidation, where Ernie is wiping his hands fastidiously on a piece of cloth and, can it be true, whistling?

'That's it, Mrs F.'

'Do you mean you've fixed it already?'

He nods modestly and reassembles the tools in his box.

'And I have lowered the temperature setting. You had it far too high.' Did I? I am speechless. Moments like this restore your faith in human nature.

Finally, we all return home to the farmhouse where I produce a gourmet lunch comprising beefburgers and potato waffles. Thank goodness the guests, for whom I cook 'wholesome meals', cannot see us now.

'Can I see Mrs Frater?'

The worried, if not alarmed, face of the farmer beckons me to the door he has just opened. He need hardly articulate the single word, 'trouble,' whispered sotto voce.

'Can I help you? It's Mrs Moss is it?' (new arrival at the cottage).

'Miss.'

Two ladies of uncertain age stand on the step. At my bidding, they step into the hall. One, taller than the other, wears her hair cropped uncompromisingly short; a cravat is knotted at the neck of her shirt, worn over straight-cut trousers and brogues. The smaller lady has silvery blue hair, curled and waved over a face of waxen white sheen, obviously well cared for. She wears a white blouse over a well-tailored tweed skirt, sheer stockings and court shoes.

'Is there anything wrong?' I begin optimistically.

'Mrs Frater, you cannot expect us to stay in that – er – place. It is quite dreadful.' She gives a slight shudder and her high-pitched voice sounds reproachful.

'What's the matter with it? I might tell you I have just spent hours cleaning the place. . . .'

'Oh, it is clean enough. It is just, well, so depressing in aspect.'

'You read the brochure I sent you' (all right - photocopied description). 'In it I do say that the accommodation is simple and basic. People come here with dogs and kids, they don't want to feel intimidated by grandeur. . . .'

'Grandeur!' Her irritating little voice almost cracks with scorn. I chose the wrong word there.

'I am sure,' she continues, 'that "types" – people such as you describe – might be glad to come and make do in your cottage.'

'Make do!' My turn to pounce on a word now. 'People like it. Come back year after year. *Love* it in fact.' I defend my cottage fiercely. The larger of the two ladies speaks for the first time. Her voice is startlingly gruff.

'The fact is, Mrs Frater, *we* do not like it and furthermore, we are *not* staying there.'

She transfers her weight from one heavily supported foot to the other and looks me in the eye. I have the unpleasant feeling that for two pins she might remove a hand from her trouser pocket and punch me between the eyes.

'I cannot help it if you haven't read the information correctly. . . .' I begin again uncertainly.

'My dear woman: "simple basic accommodation" is one thing – *that* is quite another.' She indicates vaguely in the direction of the cottage. She makes it sound like an area of inner city about to be demolished. After a few more tricky moments, the ladies present me with a ten-pound note and depart. I am left clutching the money, quivering with emotion and wondering what went wrong. You can't win 'em all.

It is clipping time. The clipping or shearing of sheep is an exercise over which the head of this household likes to make a martyr of himself. Kevin catches the ewes and rolls the fleeces, and the operation proceeds at some speed over the span of a few days.

'Well, here we are again, waiting for "cut and blow-dry". Blow-dry? That's a laugh, don't you think? I shan't be sorry to be rid of my coat this year. It's been so bloomin' hot.'

'I hope he's a bit more careful, though. I got several nicks last year. And I am a slow healer, you know.'

'How nasty! I must admit that the resultant style wasn't exactly what I had in mind – I really do fancy these modern

smooth shapes. I ended up looking a bit like a punk rocker *passée* if you know what I mean.'

'I know what you mean. I get the impression that as long as he gets it off in one piece he couldn't care a damn. He's just not interested in a girl's self-esteem – let alone the image she likes to present to the world.'

'No, all he is concerned with is getting the stuff packed, away on the lorry and waiting for the big fat cheque to roll in. They're all the same.'

'Mind you, on my last farm they had a gang. There were two or three clipping at one time, with others catching – and you really did feel as if you were on the assembly line, I can tell you. After all, here we do get the odd laugh, like when he suggested to Kevin that they have a rest. Poor soul – he is getting on you know. There he stood with sweat pouring down his face, just about collapsing – but Kevin said they couldn't stop, had to finish the pen by tea-time! I nearly wet myself at the expression on his face.'

'Oh yes, and there was the time when one of the tups didn't like the look of the set-up when he was standing in the queue, and he jumped out of the pen, only just clearing the barrier – might have cost him his malehood – and ran away.'

'Oh – oh, it's my turn next. So degrading being "styled" in that position but I have learned from experience that it pays not to struggle. Ta ta.'

Yes, the farmer staggers home at the end of a day of clipping looking like an advert for Radox Baths or Sloans Linament. He is very brave about his aches and pains though, and eases himself into a chair to await a cup of tea.

'Oh look – you've dropped the cup!'

'It's my wrist. Gone again. They always go at clipping time.' He demonstrates a pathetic gesture with a limp wrist. 'I'll have to go to the doctor.'

'You did the same thing last year. Haven't you still got those supports?'

'I suppose that they *might* be somewhere. That is if someone hasn't thrown them away.'

After his refreshment, he staggers off to search in his drawers. There are two drawers in the old chest in the back kitchen, over which I have absolutely no control. This is partly due to the fact that they have no handles and the only means of gaining entry is with the strong blade of the pen knife. Who needs locks and keys which get lost? I have the suspicion that removal of the handles has been deliberate as I have been known to consign bundles of rusting material to the dustbin, only to learn after the dustbin has been emptied that this was the vital spare part or something. Anyway, suffice to say – I have not seen the interior of either drawer for many months.

An exclamation of triumph from the next room indicates success. He holds it up for my inspection. Sheep muck may lose its flavour or effluvia over a twelve-month period but it does not look very attractive. The brown canvas and velcro 'garment' strengthened with steel supports is fitted to the wrist.

'That's better!'

'I don't care what you do with it but removal at the table would be welcome.'

'All right, all right. But don't blame me if I drop my cup – or glass. . . .'

At the end of this busy week, we have a rare social engagement. I telephone my mother.

'I've had such a bad cold this week,' she croaks. 'I've been to the vet this morning,' – hurt by my laughter – 'to have Mandy's paw seen to,' she concludes. It seems that my mother's dog has a problem similar to that of the sheep shearer.

'What did the vet say?' I enquire with interest.

'Well, he has bound it up, told me to rest her and has said she may have to have an operation in the not-too-distant future.'

'Rest! She doesn't do anything anyway! She'll get fatter than ever.'

'She's not fat. It's all hair.'

'But she has just been clipped!'

At this point, I decide that a more conciliatory tone is called for. I remember the reason for the call.

'Are you better now yourself? From your cold?'

'Improving, dear, thank you. Is everyone all right at your end?'

'Well, his lordship has had a busy week, clipping. We thought we might go out tomorrow night. There's a barn dance at. . . .'

'Oh no, not tomorrow night. I'm on the teas at the Bowls.'

'Couldn't someone else do it for a change? After all, this is the first night out we have had for ages.'

'Now, you know I don't like shirking my responsibilities.'

'You take on too much. There's your WI, the WRVS, Meals on Wheels, meals out, meals in. . . .'

'All right. I'll see what I can do. I'll phone you back.'

I know perfectly well that she would rather do 'the teas' every night for thousands of thirsty bowlers than look after her little grandchildren for an hour or two, and who could blame her? However, in the end she must have decided that an act of abstinence would be good for the soul (oh yes the Church is another of her activities – she plays the organ), and she announces in tones demanding undying gratitude that she will do the deed.

Now, we have been to quite a number of country dances over the years – well about three to be precise. They have usually been held in the hall of one of the schools, where they go under the title of ceilidhs. Only very rarely is such an event held in the barn of a local farm but in such circumstances it is called, not surprisingly, a barn dance. The music is the same, and it is usually the same performers. The school hall is taken up almost entirely with dancers, a few chairs and tables pressed to the sides of the room for a little rest and refreshment. Those present usually comprise enthusiastic parents determined to support all things associated with the school plus a hard core of country dance aficionados brought in from a radius of fifty miles or more.

It is a barn dance tonight and the comparison with the school ceilidh ends after the 'music'. For one thing, the barn is about ten times the size of the school hall, and it does not matter what you do to a barn it still looks like a barn. Whatever the time of year it feels chilly and damp, as if missing its usual many inmates deep in straw, generating warmth.

The question as you walk through the door is, where are the dancers? Is anyone dancing? The 'dance floor' occupies the final fifth of the building, the space in between being composed of the bar and its 'clients' plus a large area of people drinking, some wondering why they are there. As a rule, farmers do not like to dance, especially this sort of dancing, which they feel makes them look foolish. The farming fraternity will not be found on the dance floor but at the bar or environs, talking about tractors.

Now, it has to be recorded on these pages, where I have vowed to speak the truth that when we go to these do's, we dance. Although various complaints are made during the course of the evening – and more afterwards – of the agony experienced in elbows, knees and ankles, they are largely ignored. 'It is better for your head to *dance*,' and it is.

The directions for the dancing are given by a diminutive figure on a platform, backed by the usual fiddle, squeeze box, etc., and from time to time she leaps down and pushes people into place with a forcefulness reminiscent of a farmer sorting sheep. Nevertheless, we do-si-do and strip the willow with the best of them. Another difference between the barn dance and the ceilidh is that at the former the proceedings often become a little too bawdy for the die-hards and therefore you are less likely to be 'tutted at' if you make a mistake . . . and do we make mistakes?

Next morning: 'What is that huge multicoloured bruise on my arm? I don't remember an injury. I don't think I drank *that* much. I must get my medical reference book out – it could be leukaemia.'

'Leukaemia be blowed. And I wish you'd never bought

that book; you've had just about everything in it.'

'It wasn't my idea. You insisted on having it from *Readers' Digest* as you thought you might win a Porsche.'

'Oh, never mind. *Look* – this is why you are bruised.'

He extends his forearm towards me, encased in its splint in several shades of brown. It looks innocuous (if dirty) but of course it is reinforced with steel. I am not sure whether he wore it to ensure the strength of one joint, or as a talking point with other members of the profession. At all events, the dramatic-looking bruise remains for days and provides a talking point for its possessor.

There is one huge blot on the horizon in June. Well, not so much a blot as a cloud that comes over year after year across the North Sea. No matter how busy (with Bee and Bees and the like) or pregnant this farmer's wife might be, she has to extend the arm of British hospitality and smile brilliantly whilst she does so. A student, who worked on the farm long ago, when my in-laws received such young men from all parts of the globe, is now a lecturer in agriculture in Denmark. For a number of years now he has brought over a party of thirty to forty-five of his students to see the farming of the area.

The present incumbent of this farm has to provide a selection of dairy and pig farms for them to visit, and his wife sees to the nosebag arrangements. As if this were not enough, on the day of their arrival, she has to undertake the refreshments herself here at the home farm. This is no joke. For days beforehand I send up earnest prayers that the weather will be good, so that they can go into the garden and eat and drink al fresco.

There have been years when this has proved impossible. Not that they haven't been well-behaved. I have never seen thirty or forty pairs of shoes or clogs outside the back door before. No, it is really just a question of numbers: thirty to forty large young men, with the odd young woman, seem to take over a place somehow. They are encouraged (by guess who) to explore a typical Northumbrian farmhouse which I understand to be in sharp contrast to a Danish one, the highlights of such tours usually being the stumbling across of the odd sleeping infant.

Today, the weather is fine. I take tray after tray of filling fare such as rolls, quiches and pizzas into the garden, as well as crates of lager. I chuck out paper cups and plates for the fastidious and leave 'em to it.

I'll never forget the first time they came. They had booked a camp site on the coast, south of here, but on arriving in their huge bus did not like the site, for a reason that remains unclear. We did not discover this disquieting fact until the troubled face of their tutor appeared at the backdoor, around 7 pm.

'Well,' we began uncertainly, 'you could pitch your tents in the sand dunes tonight and look for somewhere else tomorrow.' (Our landlord does not like campers.)

'Oh no,' says he, 'you don't understand. These boys want showers, toilets, bars – *women*!'

'Oh!' Speechless, we stare at this red-faced, rather uncomfortable looking young man. He nervously lights a cigarette, inhales the smoke deeply and then declares, 'We'll sort something out. I'll tell them to get out of the bus and come and eat in your garden.' I may state here that his arrogant optimism has not diminished over the years.

Sure enough, they file past the kitchen window, laden with stores, apparently unconcerned by their predicament and, like their leader, quite confident that 'something will turn up'. And it does – but not without more than a little effort on the part of a few individuals. The problem is that although camp sites abound in the area for caravans, no one wants tents for some unspecified reason. The camp site at the end of the road was not here then and even if it had been, I doubt if it would have fulfilled all the conditions required. After a while, I have an idea – not a very good one but it is a slender ray of hope.

'I'll phone Harry.'

'What the hell is Harry going to do?'

Harry runs a hotel in the town and knows everything and everybody. His cool, efficient voice echoes smoothly down the phone.

'I'm just in the middle of serving dinners at the moment. Leave it with me.'

Somehow I feel soothed by his confident manner, although I have known him for years and realise that, in common with the rest of us, his shop front is only skin deep. We three decide to eat, Nils merely picking at his food with preoccupation. At last, the telephone rings. 'I've fixed it.' Harry tries not to sound too pleased with himself.

'What? How? Where?'

'I rang Johnson's caravan site up the road. I know Eddie Johnson pretty well. Done a few deals with him, that sort of thing. I suggested he put your people down on the football pitch. It's out of the way and no one's using it at the moment. He wasn't too keen at first but I said, ''Look, Eddie, old son, forty big Danish drinkers. Think of the bar takings, lad.'' He saw my point.'

'Harry, that is just the greatest thing. You are marvellous. You are.'

'Well, I wouldn't say that,' he demurs modestly, 'just common sense really.'

Since that night all those years ago, this caravan site has gratefully opened its gates to these thirsty campers for a few days each June, the arrangements being mutually pleasing. I have never found out about the women. I have never asked.

Now, once I have done my bit with Goswick hospitality I can relax, but my better half has the unenviable task of accompanying these boys round the farms where he has arranged visits. The actual organisation of suitable venues is not easy in this area of beef, sheep and arable farms but somehow it is done, several long-suffering dairy and pig men suffering year after year. At the end of the exhausting few days, the farmer and his wife are ceremoniously presented with a bottle of foul-tasting Danish liqueur, and we'll hear no more till next spring.

The hens are laying their eggs all over the place. It's a game that's getting me down. The most skilled exponents at this art are those new bantams that Jack sent down. One of course has become the proud mother of half a dozen bundles of joy and is, it seems, non-productive at the moment. Now that we are approaching the time of year when I desperately need my full quota of eggs, and have little time to spare to look for them, the blessed creatures start playing tricks.

We have reached the stage where in order to meet my weekly requirements for my regular round, I am having to buy in eggs for our own use. Not that it matters; this is a classical exercise in the pulling of wool over the eyes of the gullible public. The Bee and Bees see the hens running round freely outside and gobble up their Co-op eggs at breakfast with gusto: 'You can certainly tell the difference between free-range eggs and shop eggs, can't you – I never thought you could.' You have to laugh. It's times like these when a little superiority creeps in.

Anyway, one morning I glance out of the kitchen window, shortly after the hen house door has been flung wide open. There goes one of Jack's bantams. Phew, what a speed – where is she heading for? This could prove helpful. Ah, I see, she has settled down in that bunch of nettles over there. Oh-oh, that's unfortunate. She'll be right in the path of those sheep he is bringing in later for the selection committee. Must keep an eye on this. Could be fun.

'Well, you wouldn't believe it! There was I sitting, minding my own business on my nest – I am up to a dozen now – I was so pleased – they've never been able to find it – and what happens? I thought the world had come to an end. Along came thousands of those dirty woolly things, making such a row. You've never heard the like. I thought that cockerel made a racket but this was something else. Deafening. That's the only word for it. Came closer and closer; the ground was

shaking – and the smell – ugh – I just had to leave. . . .'
Sniff. Sniff.
  'There, there, dear – plenty more where those came from.'
  'I know but I've sat on that nest for days and days. I would
love a family like yours, you know. I am not going back. I
know what I'll find, their dirty big feet will have been every-
where (sniff), I'll never be the same again. I'm all of a do-dah.
It will be days before I have the strength to lay another egg.'

It certainly is noisy. The ewes and larger lambs are being
separated in the pens. Then the lambs will be poked and
prodded with a view to possible departures. Poor dears . . .
so young . . . they haven't had much of a life. . . . A short
life and a merry one, I suppose. Ah well, that seems to be it
at last. The dogs are getting ready to drive the ewes and those
not considered plump enough for the plate back to the field,
thank goodness. The chosen ones are being driven into the
garden field whilst they await the wagon.

Later the same day: a body is discovered in the garden
field. What had been a field of high-spirited youngsters –
noisily playing games, as youngsters will – is now empty
and quiet. The driver is contacted and he reports that the
death had occurred before his arrival to carry them off to
market. The mystery remains. How are we going to dispose
of the body?

The window cleaner has a shock some hours later when
he views through the now-transparent glass the dismem-
bered unfortunate (death by misadventure has been hastily
recorded) being further dissected on the kitchen table. This
sort of accident occurs from time to time, the incidence being
too sporadic to remember what we did the time before. The
resultant joints and cutlets inserted into poly bags and consigned to the freezer are rather odd in shape and bear little
resemblance to anything you are likely to see in the butcher's
shop. We are finally left with a bloodstained table and at least
one of us understanding why vegetarianism is so popular
these days.

Why should the wife of a stock farmer feel she should conceal her beliefs? I can turn out a pretty mean nut cutlet these days and as for lentilburgers or spinach roulade, well, they have to be experienced (no member of my family will volunteer to share the experience, I may add). There is no doubt about it. In this environment-conscious society with its additive awareness, more and more of us are turning towards vegetarianism.

One cynical friend of mine (also a farmer's wife, incidentally) described the triple conversion of the thinking man/-woman to vegetarianism, Catholicism and socialism. This farmer's wife is not so sure about this. She knows better than to introduce the subjects of religion or politics in her Bee and Bee relationships but she does not want the 'veggies' to feel discriminated against just because they are in a meat-producing zone. Furthermore, she fancies that vegetarian cooking is much more interesting than meat cookery.

However, we do encounter problems of conflict when we come to dietary peculiarities associated with health. We have a family staying here this weekend (mercifully for only one night), of which one member drinks neither tea nor coffee, one daughter avoids all dairy products, and another daughter is a vegetarian. You can see why I regard straight vegetarians as easy. It is quite amusing, again on health grounds, to find bacon fat neatly removed from the rasher remaining on the plates after breakfast, in the knowledge that a mountain of brandy snaps and cream has disappeared down the same alimentary tract the previous night.

To some, of course, food is of no importance, whatsoever. I do freely admit to finding these clients refreshing. Yes, this is the season of the short break – or dirty weekend as it used to be called. They come at all ages, from a variety of ethnic backgrounds and all levels of society. One might venture to suggest that a house containing a sizeable family of children would be a highly unsuitable venue for such an exercise but then, perhaps a background of continuous noise and chaos gives a certain muffling of all other movement. And after all, they can creep in and out unnoticed. From the landlady's point of view, she can relax in the knowledge that the film of dust on the window ledges will go unremarked; ditto the ring round the bath, not to mention the plastic ducks which have not been replaced, post-ablutions, in the plastic container provided. Whereas these shortcomings might appal the middle-aged matron with a silver anniversary under her wide belt, to lovers everything is quaint and romantic, even if they do notice:

'Do you remember that first weekend, darling? *Our* first weekend?'

'Oh, you mean that grotty old farmhouse on the Northumbrian coast? The place where you slipped on a plastic boat on the bathroom floor and I nearly broke my neck by tripping over a convoy of little cars outside the loo door?'

'Yes, it was hilarious, wasn't it, darling. Then, there was that dreadful lumpy bed, which we found contained bits of Lego in the mattress.'

'And do you remember, when they brought in the breakfast, an egg slid off the plate on to the floor?'

'Yes, yes – and that funny little man in the scruffy jeans – he wasn't really the farmer was he – said it was yours?'

'It was a truly wonderful weekend. I wonder if it has changed . . .?'

Yes, you cannot please 'em all. One man's meat. . . . What one finds quaint, another will find irritating – and yet another will report you to the Tourist Board. . . .

Mind you, not all romantic weekends go well. We have one young couple who book in early in the afternoon, then go to bring in their bits and pieces and sort themselves out in their room. About twenty minutes later there is the sound of running footsteps down the stairs and feminine cries of, 'You beast.' A tearful face is subsequently perceived in the car whilst the hapless, red-faced young man explains that they will not be staying after all.

* * *

We have a thinker in our midst – if not a future theologian. I am constantly being reminded by an angelic six-year-old that God is everywhere, that God is more powerful than any of us, that the world took six days to make. Then come the queries: but what did He make it from, and what did He do on the seventh? Then there was the vexed question of the ark – why did the animals go in two by two, and did they take dogs as he didn't see any on Teacher's picture? Actually, as far as he could tell, there didn't seem to be any cows or sheep either; most of the entrants seemed to be more exotic creatures like giraffes and elephants – how did they all fit in?

It wears you out, I can tell you, especially when he adds, 'Were you born then, Mummy?' It is with relief that you hear him turn back disillusioned to the cassette recorder and his favourite tape of the moment, 'The Billy Goats Gruff'. After half an hour of 'trippetty trappetting over the ricketty racketty bridge' you reach for the bottle – and not for goats' milk either.

Now, Number One Son is asked in class the definition of a suffix.

'Isn't it a breed of sheep?' he replies.

We lead a simple life.

I have a campaign to try and improve the diet of my family. I rarely resort to beefburgers these days – well, fairly rarely. As I explain to the shop assistant when I load my basket with packs of these hideous pallid discs, complete with an outsize bag of oven chips, it is probably more of a treat for me than it is for them. Instead of coaxing them to eat what I think they should eat, I just sit back whilst they rush towards me fighting over the last square inch. I am trying hard to make them eat vegetables, apart from potatoes and baked beans that is. It takes one child fifteen minutes to masticate four peas. I have found wedges of tomato secreted in the crayon box, cauliflower in the cupboard. I have witnessed choking almost sufficiently severe for medical attention.

Is it worth it I ask myself? What is more, is it worth driving myself into the ground trying to grow an assortment of tasty vegetables in the garden? Of course it is, the Bee and Bees like them. Well, some do. We can always tell the men from the boys by the amount of spinach lingering on the serving dishes. No, the spinach is not doing well in the garden either.

July

As I have stated before between these covers, holidays are not for us – not now. Actually, now I come to think about it, perhaps that was why he was so keen to have so many children. . . . He was always reluctant to leave his beloved acres when we did go away. I used to have an awful job 'arranging things' like passport, photos, etc., not to mention the financing of the holiday itself. Then, naturally, all the packing was left to me. 'If we both do bits of packing, we'll forget something, because one will think the other has packed it.'

By the time I had finished, I was in even more need of a holiday than ever and, quite honestly, the holiday I booked in a Mediterranean villa, although some degrees warmer than the Goswick mean, usually turned out to be the mere swapping of sinks (and that *awful* plumbing . . .). Oddly enough, once we reached our distant destination, he was the one who seemed instantly able to relax, put his feet up and lose himself in one of the books so thoughtfully packed, soaking up the local vintage, even if it was not 'a patch on Scottish and Newcastle'. (He also made reference to the classic dish, paella – 'give me a plate of egg on baked beans any day'.)

By the time he was speeding back up the A1 from the airport humming 'Home Sweet Home', he looked really rejuvenated – whilst his wife in the back with the kids and tummy bugs was wondering why she had done it. Anyway, with all these children 'you insisted on having' holidays are no longer a practical proposition. Unless of course we are presented with free tickets to the Royal Show.

Here we are then. Again I ask myself it it's worth it, as I

dash round damply in the heat, assembling requirements for a 2–3 day trip, trying to cover all eventualities. The younger family members have never witnessed such a spectacle, never seen their nearest relative with wild-eyed determination trying to close an overstuffed suitcase by fair means or foul. Come to think of it, they have never seen a suitcase.

'For God's sake, put that down. Oh no – you've mixed up all my piles. . . .'

'Mummy, why are you crying?'

'Oh – it's all right. Why don't you run along and do something else – anything . . . watch 'Neighbours', pull the legs off a fly. . . .'

Silence follows this outburst and I make progress at last. But then I wonder what they are doing. Better investigate. Mmmmmmm. I suppose the sight of a toddler, clad only in a bra and rosary beads might be amusing, another time, another place. Definitely one for the album anyway – if only I could find the camera.

'Where are you going to stay?' I hear you ask, wondering what unsuspecting relative has a home large enough. The answer is that we have no such relative, not one within a reasonable radius of the Royal Show anyway. My poor cousin, her long-suffering husband and two grown-up children (plus large dog which has an aversion to small children) will be delighted to have us in their two-and-a-half bedroomed semi north of Birmingham. She said so. I am not going to worry my hot head about the logistics, she was always better at maths than I was anyway. We are going there. We are going to the Royal Show. Beyond that I am not prepared to think.

At last we are all in the car. It is stiflingly hot. I must have all the windows open but it doesn't seem to make much difference.

'Sit still and be quiet all of you.'

Fat chance. They are so excited.

'How far is it?'

'Are we nearly there?'

'No,' says the patient voice from the driver's seat, 'we've only just passed the turn for Holy Island.'

This is not going to be an easy trip. I should have given them a double – or better still, a treble – dose of travel sickness pills. The chemist said that they had a sedative effect. He was not, of course, reckoning with the constitution of a child bred to live without sleep. Why is it, I used to wail, that everyone has babies who sleep through the night from the age of six weeks, whilst I have children who still fail at this seemingly simple feat at six years – and more?

'They'll settle down,' asserts the voice from the wheel with confidence. Eventually, we reach the motorway. Where does all this traffic come from? It is unbelievable. Lorry after lorry, car after car. They all cluster for miles in front of us on the road snaking across the countryside in the shimmering heat of midsummer. At least we seem to be moving faster now, the needle of the speedometer never faltering below 70 mph. This is the stuff – soon be there at this rate.

'I want to go to the toilet!'

'So do I.'

'Well, you'll have to wait till the services.'

'What does that mean?'

'It means toilets, shops, cafés, petrol and things.'

'Oh great – can we *buy* something?'

As if we could squeeze even so much as a sliver of chewing gum into this vehicle, crammed tightly with humanity – and essential commodities like nappies, transformer toys and suitcases!

We fail to reach the services. We have to detour off the motorway at the next turning, and thereafter into a gateway through which a giggling group disappear, glad of the diversion.

Back in the car, phew, it is hot. I am sure it is getting hotter the further south we speed.

'Shall I drive for a bit, dear?'

'No, I am fine.'

At least, when driving, he does not have to deal with the assortment of requests from the rear, ranging from liquid refreshment (in carefully measured amounts) to answering questions concerning complex road signs (everything has changed since I studied the *Highway Code* for my driving test). At last, with relief, we turn off the motorway. I am sure that they are very necessary and indispensable to modern life but I find actually driving on one harrowing in the extreme.

My cousin looks pleased to see us. We are all pleased to see them.

'Sorry but we have to go out.'

'What's that? I don't blame you. To your keep fit class? In this heat?'

She and her daughter disappear in their leotards. I cannot help the feeling that such exercise will prove quite redundant in view of the effort she is going to have to make over the next few days. Her good-natured husband dispenses drinks for us all in varying strengths and quantities, and by some miracle the children disperse through the house and garden, some watching TV as if they have never seen one before and some locating the boxes of toys so thoughtfully prised out of the loft for our use. Don't ask me where we are all going to sleep.

Next morning, amazingly refreshed after a night in my cousin's comfortable bed with youngsters adjacent or in cot provided, I feel ready for anything. I am not going to delve too deeply into the sleeping arrangements of my cousin's family (they are pleased to see us, they said so); I have a feeling that something in the nature of a bivouac might have been erected in the sitting room. The older boys are thrilled to have been inserted into their sleeping bags in the conservatory, camping-style. It works well. (It is a tale I shall recount to a friend or two who declare with confidence that their house is far too small to accommodate guests.) To enhance my enjoyment further, by the time 'the little people' and I descend to the kitchen, the others have already breakfasted and no trace remains. This *is* a holiday.

At last, off we go in the car again to join the many queues for the Royal Agricultural Show.

'Have you all got your hats? And did I rub everyone with high-factor sun cream?'

'You fuss too much.'

We are flagged into a slot in the car park.

'You will never remember where it is.'

'So what? We'll worry about that when the time comes.'

Lose the car? We are more likely to lose a child, and attractive though that thought might be on occasion, one has to think in terms of the consequences. . . .

'Come back. Don't run so far ahead. Wait for us. Stick together!'

The entrance gate is negotiated with ease and we stand at a sort of crossroads, with signs pointing in all directions. Do we want to see the equestrian events? The machinery? Town and country exhibits?

'I know. I'll go and look at the tractors and equipment with the big boys and you can trundle the double push-chair around – er – elsewhere – and we'll meet at the cattle at 1 pm.'

Sounds great! Whose idea was this? As anyone who has been in the position of pushing a double push-chair any distance knows, it is hard work and you are limited in your choice of venues. How many more irritable legs am I going to hit? Sorry! There are hundreds of thousands of legs here – in all shapes and sizes. I think I'll just sit down on this seat for a moment and survey the scene.

'You sit still. I'll get you an ice lolly in a minute.'

One pair of eyes is mercifully closed. Yes, I enjoy watching examples of my fellow earth creatures file past at varying paces. On this sweltering July day, the entire range of human apparel can be seen. There are actually a few florid gentlemen in pin-striped suits and bowler hats. There are matching mates in creations of silk, legs encased in the sheerest of stockings tottering around on slim heels, many such an ensemble topped off with a crown of tulle (there is little breeze to blow it off, that's for sure).

At the other end of the range, there are those of either sex in shorts or . . . almost nothing at all. In between, a variety of combinations of shirts, slacks, cotton dresses, sandals, etc. Correspondingly, skin tones (of our compatriots, that is – for there is quite a cosmopolitan crowd here) vary from 'factor'-protected lily white through shades of weatherbeaten brown to bright rose red, indicating some sore backs tonight.

I wander on throughout the morning, gazing at charity tents, fashion shows (glimpsed through the open doorway of the tent), stalls extolling the virtues of organic produce and self-sufficiency, demonstrations of sheep shearing, spinning, milking sheep, cheese-making. . . .

In the distance, is that a pipe band I can hear? I had better start looking for the sign marked 'Cattle' as it must be nearing lunchtime. My blood sugar level feels alarmingly low; my spirits not far behind.

'Look there's Mummy!'

'Do you know what we've seen?'

'We've seen a machine for making. . . .'

'Lovely, dear.'

Well, they seem to have had a successful morning. I am glad about that, I really am.

'Are you coming round the cows then?'

Do I have to? 'Of course, I'd love to. How fascinating!'

The only consolation is that the poor creatures look even hotter than I feel, their great bodies heaving in the heat, no matter how many hosing downs they have received from their fond carers (perhaps we could have a quick shower too?)

I never realised there were so many breeds. I am glad that bull is tethered securely. I don't think he likes the look of me, I certainly don't like the look of him – perhaps his expression is merely embarrassment at having a name like that! Yes, I am interested in cattle, at times. Look at those Herefords, so friendly with their homely faces encased in all those curls.

I adore Jerseys and Guernseys. I do wish he wouldn't sneer when I say that; well, they have such lovely faces. The highlight has to be the Dexters, though; we could have a whole herd of those in that 'new' field in front of the house. Think of the prestige! The public would love it. The sneer is replaced by a snort any Aberdeen Angus would be proud of. I can't help it if these ideas come to me, it's better than being purely passive, surely.

Then a low-budget scenario springs to mind: someone milking a cow on three-cornered stool, appropriately clad of course, complete with frilly cap. That would bring 'em in droves.

'Yes, dear. I think we've seen enough cattle. We'll go along to a stand where we know someone and look hungry' (not hard to do).

They seem delighted to see us; it's part of their job of course. I do wish the children would behave. They don't seem to like any of the fare on offer so *we* eat it all (with the whispered promise of crisps, etc., soon) and at last, replete, proceed along yet another uninspected avenue.

What is this? O happiness. O joy. Children's Corner! Under the blessed shade of trees there is a collection of small pens containing rabbits, poultry, small creatures for small people to observe at close quarters. Then there are swings and slides, all the components of the average play park. Best, of all, there are wide wooden benches where mums and dads can sit in relative comfort, glass in hand, ostensibly watching the antics of their offspring. I think we'll stay here for quite a while. Hello – I never realised turkeys could move quite so fast.

'Stop that. You are not supposed to chase the poor creatures. Nor are you to poke your ice lolly sticks through the wires at the rabbits.'

It is so peaceful here for us, if not for the above-mentioned creatures, while the rest of the world still rushes by regardless. I suppose if you have paid for your ticket, you feel you have to get your money's worth, but trying to see everything in this huge showground is surely impossible – rather like our friends from across the Atlantic who 'do' their UK tour in a week.

At last, we wend our way slowly back to the car park, temporarily mislaying a couple of kids in the process. Well, that's our Royal Show for the next ten years, if past frequency is anything to go by.

The following day we spend recharging our batteries before our long journey back up the motorway. Funny how we get back more quickly than we went. I wonder what has happened in our absence?

It hardly seems fair that after sniffing and sneezing all winter from the usual succession of viruses, some sneeze all summer too. The head of the household has his hindquarters pierced with a needle laden with long-acting, relief-giving serum, and thereafter his symptoms are slight.

Number One Son, however, also afflicted, has to resort to spoonfuls of stuff from a bottle, guaranteed not to make the patient drowsy. Poor soul, he has a pathological hatred of pills, and when someone suggests a homeopathic cure from the health food shop in preference to *chemicals* (that dirty word), he has to be bribed in order to ingest the tiny white pills. Even so, half-sucked small discs are subsequently discovered in various known hiding places, after the caches of much-maligned vegetables in the former health drive. His hay fever does not improve. He has to resort to the bottle once more.

On the subject of chemicals, it is now sheep-dipping time and the all-pervasive pong fills the air, almost palpably.

'We've had a good morning. Two hundred through.'

'Er – I thought they were supposed to stay in the stuff for a minute.'

'Look – perhaps *you* would like to try keeping the dashed things swimming around in that stuff for a whole minute?'

I don't like his tone but later, after washing five reluctant heads in the bath, sympathise.

No sooner has the dipping been completed when Mandy, my mother's dog, accidentally takes a wrong turning and ends up in the sewerage ditch. I should explain that mother is on holiday and whenever she takes leave of her beloved cottage in the village where her presence is so much a part, we are the lucky recipients of her dumb companion. Mandy is a dear old thing, really. She is no trouble, well not much, as long as it is dry outside, preventing her from embellishing my floors with her large footprints – or if she does not fall into sewerage ditches.

She is going deaf now, – poor soul, with the selective deafness of the elderly. She can hear a tin being opened at one hundred yards but she no longer barks at a caller coming to the door, neither does she come when called after making her late-night ablutions. On the occasion in question we are blissfully unaware of her malodorous state until she comes waddling in quite late at night.

'Oh, my God, what are we going to do?' I wail.

'Shut her in the TV room until morning.'

He is a master of the art of not-panicking, a much under-estimated attribute, not to be sniffed at.

The first person up next morning advances warily towards the TV room, cloth over nose, and encourages the unfortunate to jump out of the window for her morning constitutional.

We have such a nice genteel family staying for the week whose children eat everything and never leave a mark on the tablecloth. It is unnatural, if not unnerving. Anyway, it is obviously in my interest and theirs to conceal this olfactory experience. I return to the Centre of Operations, whence I dispense the breakfasts and subsequently consider the next move. It is obviously a job which requires two pairs of hands.

'It's a pity I'm not still dipping,' he mutters as he lifts the offensive creature into the back kitchen sink.

'I knew I would find a use for that highly scented shampoo I bought by mistake months ago.'

Mandy wears a very strange expression on her hairy face as she stands shaking in the sink. Bucket after bucket of water is poured over her rotund form and lather after lather of what might best be described as 'mixed bouquet'. At last, a somewhat crestfallen creature is towelled down and then positioned in the yard for a natural blow-dry.

'Don't you dare do that again!' I shout into each ear.

As if he has not seen enough water for one week, it is a child's birthday on Saturday and he takes no less than nine boys swimming at the pool in town. This is pretty heroic stuff you must admit, and as he loads the car with humanity, armed with rolls of towel, he cannot resist wearing a martyred air. It looks as if that might be all he is wearing as, not long after they have left, I notice the untidy bundle of his swimming trunks and towel reposing on the kitchen chair.

An alarming picture springs to my mind. Luckily we have two cars. I fling baby and toddler in the back and dash off into town with great speed, temporarily absenting myself from the site of the welcoming committee for the holiday cottage arrivals. The girl at the pool seems quite understanding as a breathless, red-faced matron rushes towards her, waving a tubular towelling parcel.

The strawberry crop – such as it was – is as good as finished. I can subcontract this job out these days although my assistants do tend to have a vested interest in the product, and the bowls they bring into the house are barely half-full. They call themselves 'graders'. Each fruit picked is tried and if it is sweet, it is eaten; if not, it is placed, slightly 'shop-soiled' into the bowl. Ah well, with a good wash and a dollop of cream they'll be all right.

Then there are the raspberries. I am assured of a larger crop here since they are less sweet. On the other hand, since the job is less attractive, it is soon abandoned. The blackcurrant picking I always do alone.

As it is a good year for these fruits, I subsequently have the problem of what to do with the wretched things once picked. There is a limit to the number of guises in which they can be served to the Bee and Bees: raspberry pavlova, raspberry crumble, blackcurrant pie. If the raspberries are not choice enough for freezing, you are left with the unavoidable course, jam-making.

Now, with the fruits of winter and spring I can produce a passable preserve, but with the sweet fruits of summer. . . .

'For goodness sake, don't tip that jar like that!'

'It's the best way of pouring it on to my bread. Why don't we use it on ice cream as well?'

The trouble with runny jam is that although it goes further and tastes fresher, it inclines to mould more quickly. Therefore it does end up in the above serving suggestion or, if a burst of industry comes on, in that popular confection, jam tarts!

I don't know which is worse, the kitchen or the garden. Back in the latter the courgettes are thriving. To my astonishment, every single seedling grown after the 'mousey' business survived – and I grew a lot, determined to demonstrate who is boss around here. Yes, there is nothing like the growing of these vegetables, they seem to increase in stature almost before your eyes. I know I have watered them but once established, heat seems to be the prerequisite, and heat is what they have had this summer. Therefore, we now have about thirty bushes beginning to sprout large, unreal-looking yellow flowers in profusion.

'I think you have overdone it this year, dear. You know I cannot stand the things anyway.'

I saw a programme on television once where the flowers were served on the plate as a delicacy. Perhaps not. I know where to draw the line.

Well, the Bee and Bees like courgettes anyway, served as part of my home-grown-without-chemicals meals. Another attraction is that they are wonderfully easy to pick. A handful of decent-sized vegetables and there you have it! Unlike the peas and beans, where a considerable amount of back-breaking garnering creeps in. . . . And, another thing – a glut is preferable to a famine, isn't it?

Naturally, my hens, which I proudly describe to people as

ranging free, do. Unfortunately, their territory seems frequently to include the garden. This behaviour irritates the gardener more than somewhat, who feels that she simply cannot win. There is interference to her precious plants before planting and no sooner are they starting to look hopeful, when they are attacked from another angle. Bantam mother has now left her brood to fend for themselves and is espied frolicking in the fruit bushes with Bantam cockerel.

The saying, 'all the world loves a lover' has its exceptions and this is one of them. I chase them out, the children chase them out, everyone chases them out, still they keep coming. There is obviously something very special about their love bower between the blackcurrant bushes. I wouldn't mind if they stayed there but I know from bitter experience that they soon get bored with each other's company and start raking round my young flowers and vegetables. Anyone peering over the wall on a sunny summer evening might be startled to see a grim-faced farmer's wife on all fours stalking an apparently innocent small hen through the bushes. Paranoid – moi?

The sight of the office table in the middle of the lawn, littered with greasy plates and dirty glasses, one bright and sunny morning is an unusual one. It has rained during the night, which has the overall effect of making the picture look even less attractive. In the corner, by the wall, there is a black plastic bag bulging with empty bottles and cans. There are charred bones, which even the cottage cats fail to find appealing. Yes, we had a barbecue last night; we must have done, although my feelings are a little confused on the subject.

'We'll just leave everything till tomorrow,' someone said (was it me?) as we laughed in the darkness and groped our way into the house where we resumed our discussions in comfort. It was great fun – I think.

'Have a good barbecue?' the bed and breakfast guest enquires cheerfully. 'Where is he this morning?'

'Er – he has a headache.'

'Ha – I thought it sounded as if it was developing into a liquid evening. Ha ha.'

Why do people have to shout so? Our guest attacks his muesli with even greater gusto, obviously feeling in the pink this morning, whilst others are feeling blue, or even a trifle green.

'My God,' exclaims Evelyn. 'Well, it makes a change, I suppose,' as she carries tray after tray of dirty dishes and glasses into the kitchen. Barbecues in this country are always unusual, we rarely get a sufficiently long period of suitable weather to perfect the technique. Therefore, in the first spell of really hot, settled weather, we drag out the rusting and rather disgusting-looking apparatus, from where it has been lurking since last year – or was it the year before?

We purchase a bag of charcoal and announce we are having a barbecue. Everyone brings their own ingredients: sausages, spare ribs, chops, lentilburgers . . . once some enthusiastic chef has had his greasy hands on the stuff, I defy anyone to tell the difference. Yes, our barbecues are great equalisers, a prime steak can taste exactly the same as a sausage – burnt! In order to eat these dubious-looking offerings, a reasonable degree of alcoholic anaesthesia is recommended, if not obligatory. No, these affairs are not for the abstainer, or even the moderate.

Notwithstanding this, it is bound to have been something I ate which has made me feel so ill this morning. Well – I mean, it could have been anything.

Ah well – as a once-a-year occasion, it was good fun. Unfortunately, one of the chefs has had to sort out lambs for market this morning, a job he normally enjoys and speeds through with ease. Not today. Subsequently, quite a squad come home rejected, tail between legs, and on inspection, he seems surprised he ever sent them.

If an abandoned barbecue is a sorry sight in the morning, what I am about to describe is a thousand times worse. It is a glorious mid-summer morning, perfect in fact. The birds are singing and the sun has been shining from a cloudless sky since its first appearance.

Scene: kitchen
Enter Number One Son from the garden
N.O.S. There are six heifers in the garden
Me What! You're joking?
N.O.S. No – it's true. Kevin went into the garden field to feed his pet lambs and there they were. He thinks they must have jumped over the ha ha.

All this sounds uncomfortably possible. The field is bare and doubtless some of my watered greenery looked attractive. *Six*? Number One Son is not given to hyperbole. Now, had it been Number Two Son, I might have expected to see one tiny calf or a cow leaning its head over the gate, but no – this sounds serious. I am not sure I feel strong enough to take it. My legs tremble as I follow my firstborn into the garden, shading my eyes against the glare of the sun. I don't want to look. Be brave!

Sure enough, at the bottom of the garden are six extremely large and lively ladies. A worried looking Kevin is leaping around and waving a stick trying to chase them out; in his wake are a number of small boys, including his own, all cheering and shouting. I do declare that they are actually enjoying this occasion.

At last, five of the intruders have taken their exit. One remains, determined not to quit. Looking scornfully after her departing sisters, she kicks her heels and trots past the human fence, headed by Kevin. My poor precious little daughter, inexperienced in the art of stockmanship stands alone and terrified in the middle of the lawn. The heifer charges towards her, whilst we stand powerless in horror. A piercing scream suddenly echoes all round the garden, and miles beyond I shouldn't wonder. The creature skids to a halt, looking terrified in turn, and off she goes in the other direction.

I scoop up the screamer and after a second or two to gather her wits, the animal circumnavigates the garden again. All the time this is going on, I am trying not to look at my vegetable plots and flower beds, at which I have worked so hard. . . . Kevin looks more upset every minute. I don't know which he fears the most, the cow or the farmer's wife with her set expression and mutterings of revenge and divorce at least.

At last, the lady calls it a day, feeling she can do no more damage this morning. We all withdraw from the scene of the crime, exhausted by our labours. When 'Daddy' returns cheerfully whistling from his pleasant walk in the sunshine round his stock, they all fight to be first with the news.

'Oh, dear,' he says, 'I wondered where they were.'

He marches off into the garden to inspect the damage, returning with the news that, 'It's not too bad . . . could be worse. . . .' I dare say it could – we could have had the whole herd, plus bull and four or five hundred sheep.

Eventually I gather the courage to examine closely for myself the result of the morning's activities. It is easy to follow the route they took. A straight line through the rose bed, dislodging the ornamental edging stones as they go, through the children's garden, resting perhaps for a few minutes in the herb garden to sample a few interesting flavours. Then it looks as if they did a sort of dance through the peas and beans; they didn't waste much time on the courgettes ('see – even the cows don't like them'); they finished off the strawberries and flattened the raspberries at their peak of production. Finally – where have all the potatoes gone?

It could have been worse! When I think of the hours I have spent weeding and watering. . . . I could weep . . . I shall weep. There is only one minute crumb of comfort I can find in this pitifully barren waste – the activities of the mice and hens have certainly paled into insignificance.

They have started cutting the winter barley. We have used contractors for this job for some years now, ever since, in fact, our last combine went up in flames – luckily late in the season. I may say that I had been advocating the use of contractors for ages before that, but experience is slowly teaching that it takes at least five years before the words of an ignorant, urban-born female are able to take root. Balanced against the usual disadvantages, the hours he and Kevin have spent knee-deep in parts, covered in oil and *still* having to send for the expert simply had to win the argument in the end. The fact that the contractor takes the burden on to his broad shoulders, somehow makes the whole procedure less painful.

Nevertheless, it is still exciting and stressful to discover what sort of crop you have managed to rear, what sort of yield and, most importantly, what you are going to get for it. This last necessitates a number of phone calls, the conversation spiced with the 'agrispeak' which is so confusing for we lesser mortals to follow. Who would have thought that the tiny seed of life looked at on the palm of your hand could be the subject of so many arguments and contain fascinating things like Hagberg and moisture contents. The latter is mercifully low this year so there will not be the exorbitant drying charges of other years to strip the icing from the cake.

Even so, we hardly seem to be making loads of money – in the way that 99 per cent of the population seems to think. And, good harvest it might be, but this farmer's wife fails to get excited for the simple reason that he just goes out and buys another few hundred ewes or a tractor. On the other hand, in bad years past, she has been the lucky recipient of government munificence – right into her purse. Funny old world isn't it?

However, back to the income I understand, the Bee and Bees. We are in full throttle with a steady succession of casuals (one-nighters en route to Scotland), interspersed with the bookings.

A lone walker suddenly appears at the door. We are too far off the main road to have many of these. Most of our clients come telephoned through the tourist board or through its excellent little booklet.

Anyway, here she is, this lady. She looks normal, and announces she is walking part of the coast. She seems glad of our hospitality and to have a captive audience, and although it is only afternoon, decides to treat her weary limbs to a soak. It is rather unfortunate that someone has recently unscrewed the knobs from some of the doors when there wasn't much on TV and a screwdriver had been carelessly left in view.

Apparently, quite some time elapses before one of the children hears a 'mayday call' coming from within the bathroom. Not given to sensationalism, he comes downstairs and calmly announces he has 'let a woman out of the bathroom'. How? He found that the handle of *our* bedroom door was loose; he removed it and inserted it where required.

I am mortified, but luckily the lady in question has a sense of humour and was not in a hurry. Thereafter, I resolve to fix that door once and for all, particularly as I anticipate my other guests tonight could be a little more precise. I am not wrong.

Unfortunately, I have a bad night with one teething and one wheezing, and overshoot my estimated time of rising; add to this the fact that the couple concerned take their places in the dining room even earlier than stated and you have a problem. A dash into the dining room reveals the absence of cereal bowls, which I hastily rectify. I then discover I have forgotten to buy sausages or get dressed – and we are out of milk (and of course the milkman is late). An elegantly plucked eyebrow is raised at my state of dress.

When the delicious hour of their departure arrives there is no change for their proffered notes, despite ransacking the children's piggy banks.

'That's all right,' the smartly dressed lady smiles (what a complexion – she obviously does not live where the full force of the north-east wind can remove the top layer of skin every time the door is opened). 'Leave it in credit as we would like to stay with you again on our way home.' I am speechless.

We try to make it a policy to ask the night before what sort of breakfast people might require. As previously stated, when guests go into the dining room in the mornings, the table should be already set with cereals, milk, juice, etc., so that if they shun the great British breakfast they can just get on with it without further bother to the poor landlady.

A doctor, his wife and four children book in for the night. They are just Bee and Bee, as opposed to Bee, Bee and Ee, and not terribly forthcoming – so somehow, they slip through the net the night before. They are perceived pacing up and down outside the dining room from 7.45 onwards. Backstage, I am going through all my usual activities like burning the bacon, throwing windows open wide, breaking eggs, etc.

The breakfast waiter is on the receiving end of a few choice comments as he dances around whispering sotto voce 'they're *there*.' At last, I have a beautifully arranged platter of bacon, sausages, tomatoes, mushrooms and six perfectly poached eggs nestling upon their triangles of crisply fried bread. He is just leaving the starting blocks; he is off – when a face flags him down:

'I forgot to mention: only one of us eats eggs.'

The cook at this stage has to be physically restrained by the breakfast waiter from hurling the other five at the face. Thus thwarted, she removes five from the plate, their future undecided. She proceeds to carry the now somewhat denuded ashet into the dining room herself, dispensing with the services of the waiter, who follows nervously a few feet behind. The breakfast is then slammed noisily down on to the hot plate, without ceremony or words, and the family is treated to a long look, guaranteed to freeze the remaining breakfast components and hopefully impair their digestion for the rest of the day.

Next, we have another booking. Mr Jones is here for a week, having come up from the south determined to have a holiday without the aid of the motor car. His strength has to be admired. It is not easy if you want to go any further afield than the shore, because you have to retrace your steps back and forth the three miles to the main road. This does not seem to worry Mr Jones.

He has brought an extraordinary amount of luggage, obviously thinking that the weather will be cold or wet. This year, however, it is hot – to the surprise of Mr Jones. Every evening, he returns even browner than the day before until, by the end of the week, he blends into the deep polished mahogany of the dining room table, where he frequently eats in splendid isolation.

Mr Jones is friendly and pleasant but he has come here for a holiday of solitude and we respect his privacy. Give the public what they want. Peace is tricky in a family of these proportions but when he leaves, Mr Jones declares his holiday to have been perfect. At such a moment, it all seems worthwhile.

After Mr Jones we have a family with a dog. We do not mind dogs as long as they don't bark too much, bite or chase sheep, and this dog does none of these things. He is not a clever dog, though. On an educational walk round the ancient walls of Berwick, he falls off and breaks a leg. '. . . and so,' the voice concludes apologetically on the telephone later on the day of their departure, '. . . could we come back and stay another night?'

I repress a violent urge to scream down the phone as, of course, in the interim, I have wasted a good deal of time and energy between beds, washing machine and washing-line. 'That will be fine, Mr McDougall,' I hear myself say brightly because I have just remembered something else. When I made out their bill this morning, I made an error and undercharged them by a not-inconsiderable amount. They did not correct me and I had written it off subsequently with the 'c'est la vie and I'll be more careful in future' philosophy I am learning to adopt in this business. However, perhaps a little readjustment can now be made? The dog will not be boarding at this establishment tonight as he has been detained under medical supervision till tomorrow.

So we press on through the month until we reach the final week, which is always reserved for the golfers. You might think that, living so near a golf course, we might do business with a fair sprinkling of such sportsmen. Not so. We do have the odd 'fun player' of course but generally speaking, the golfer likes to hang his hat in a more salubrious establishment than this. However, during the last week of July, a tournament is held here which attracts participants from all over northern Britain. Many years ago, a couple of young boys from Durham decided that a house within drinking distance of the clubhouse was desirable; they were soon joined by another . . . and another. . . . When one night, giggling, they roused another guest in the early hours by aiming objects at his window as they thought the door was locked (which it was not) I vowed to reserve this week exclusively for golfers.

This has paid off. The two originals now bring their wives and several fellow players and friends from home. They do not require any attention once breakfast is over, though some mornings breakfast is more popular than others. Golfers law: late night before equals little catering next morning. 'Nerves is it?' suggests the breakfast waiter sympathetically as the young man stares accusingly at his cornflakes.

'No, it's not nerves,' is the honest answer, 'and I'll not have anything cooked this morning, thank you.' Yes, their serious sport is punctuated with blasts of revelry – and why not? They come to enjoy themselves.

One new addition to the team has a video camera. This seemingly inoffensive item spells bad news for the busy landlady and her assistant, eager to *get on*. If the players do not have to be off the tee early, they take extra cups of coffee after breakfast and adjourn to the TV room to watch the previous day's play. Must have been good – loud guffaws echo through the house. . . . Evelyn and I exchange glances.

The week passes swiftly. They all stay as long as someone remains in the tournament. This year, one reaches the final on the last day. They are happy. I am happy. Each day they all stay clicks up more on the credit side of my accounts (well, it would if I did accounts). Alas – he loses but I am still happy for, had he won, perhaps they would not have returned the following year for their holiday.

August

'Have you any eggs to spare, Mrs F?' asks Samson, with a large and meaningful wink. It is Friday night and he loads his van with two or three dozen and grins. As it happens, at this time of year many of my regular clients are away on holiday so I am happy to make 'temporary alternative arrangements'.

What comes next is that we have a chapter of accidents in the Bee and Bee department, like the timer being sabotaged by a disinterested party so that the order of six soft boiled eggs has to be repeated. It is therefore with not so much surprise as concern that I regard my nearest and dearest on all fours half inside a bush in the shrubbery; the bantams are hiding their eggs again.

'Don't worry, dear. I'll just have to buy some from the Co-op again.'

The builders are back – and how! You may not believe this but for years we have lived in this dilapidated old farmhouse uncomplaining. We have not really noticed the rotten woodwork inside and out, broken spouts, crumbling rendering, cracked chimney pots, disintegrating plasterwork, etc.

It has crossed my mind on more than one occasion that this is not the warmest house on this earth, but I have put this down to position and an antiquated central heating system. In any case 'some people' do not like warm houses – so there!

However, suddenly, out of the blue, we have a series of visitations right down the hierarchy. First the landlord, then the agent, then the buildings expert, then the building supervisor. Something is obviously in the wind. There are a lot of mutterings about 'improvements'. The last visitor on the list has a sad face and, after a detailed tour of inspection, arrives back in the kitchen, shaking his head mournfully. I consider offering him my hanky. Eventually, he gives a watery smile and mumbles, 'We'll do our best.'

He talks on a little to my husband in builderspeak and I half-listen uncomprehending, and quite frankly, hardly interested. However, when I catch the odd phrase like 'internal plasterwork', I prick my ears. This cannot be true? He cannot be serious? Not now surely? I gather, with increasing incredulity that this job is about to start at any minute and will last weeks if not months! Oh – no, no, no – NO! Why do radical surgery now on a house which has been in a chronic condition for years?

'Don't worry, dear,' says my husband soothingly after the departure of the building supervisor. I am sitting at the table in an advanced state of shock and despair. They could not have picked a more inconvenient time; August is by far the busiest month in the Bee and Bee department and I have less help because of the 'wretched harvest'.

'At least it will be Samson and Them,' my husband concludes. 'It could be worse'. This is one of the qualities of his nature which I find irritating or uplifting in turns. I daresay it could be worse: 'they' could have decided to raze the whole place to the ground in August, I suppose. . . .

Yes, the work starts straight away. Outside first, thank goodness. Here they come, Samson and Them. Samson's assistant, though hardly a shrinking violet, does not appear to have a name. The duo are known throughout the district as 'Samson and Them' rather like Laurel and Hardy or perhaps Tweedledum and Tweedledee. They sit at the kitchen table, outlining the proposed arrangements. I groan.

'How about if we just knocked the whole lot down and built you a nice bungalow – all on the flat – easily run – Mrs F?' Samson suggests. I manage to swallow strong feelings I have about nice bungalows or modern houses in general.

I am only too painfully aware that you can get away with

a lot in a crumbling ruin. For a start, by the very size of the building, the mess inevitably accrued from the numbers of occupants has more room to disperse. The untidiness is not all confined to one or two rooms. There are obsolete rooms like the dairy or the office where you can hide clutter if it gets on top of you. Also, you can get away with doing little in the way of work. I find that strategically placed plants and flowers work wonders in creating that 'cared for' look; plaster the kitchen walls with children's drawings and add the occasional hand-thrown pot, and what you have is the slightly-arty-folksy look. Now, in a smaller, modern house, you have to work hard, mopping, polishing, tidying – you even have to keep the windows clean. . . .

No, Samson, thank you very much. You just do what you've been instructed to do. It could not have come at a worse time but, that's life, and we'll endeavour to put up with it. How brave I am being. Ah, here comes the farmer, fresh from his rounds.

'Do you always leap up and make him a cup of coffee like that, Mrs F. when he comes in?' enquires Samson with interest.

'No, he usually makes it himself.'

'My wife makes me a cup of tea or coffee when she has hers – and then heats it up in the microwave when I come in.'

O Technological Age – what a lot you have to answer for!

Samson and Them finish their coffee and then move outside to plan their day's strategy. Before we know where we are there is what the children call a 'climbing frame' erected outside the back door and work begins. We start from the top apparently. It is quite unnerving to be pegging out the washing, with the slow dawning of realisation that you are being watched from above by two figures crouched on the roof, ruminatively rolling cigarettes and . . . thinking. Slowly but surely, things start to happen, like removal of redundant chimney pots, since it is in their brief to fill in fireplaces.

'You'll be able to put plants in these in the yard, Mrs F,' suggests Samson, helpfully.

That is an idea. The yard certainly does need brightening up but fortunately this project would be better deferred until next year. . . . I do feel that the scaffold at the back door does detract from the overall quaintness of the place. Guests are asked to use the front door for their entrances and exits but in common with most farmhouses I know, the backdoor is the one met first. These houses were built in the days of the servant when tradesmen would come to the back door automatically from the road.

Luckily, the work in hand over the coming weeks is confined to the back of the house. Therefore, although first impression of the house will be poor, we hope to compensate quickly with our charm, comfort and good food in the front of the house. That's the theory.

Samson and Them know everyone. I glance through the window and am startled to see the coalman apparently talking to himself, standing in the middle of the yard. No, it's Them on the roof engaging him in local gossip. The same thing happens with the baker. Life goes on relatively unscathed inside. We relax and enjoy snatches of Samson's commentary and philosophy.

Oh – oh, things are getting serious now. Samson and Them are coming inside. 'Have you any old sheets, Mrs F?'

Do I have any other kind? The Bee and Bee beds are decked out in duvets, whether they like it or not. I am therefore able to furnish Samson and Them with some sheets to protect floor and furniture during the improvements. I cannot help wailing at intervals (though I do try to restrict it to once or twice daily). If only the powers that be had decided to raise the quality of our life during the period from September to April when we could have spread through the house – leaving them to it! As it is, we are imprisoned in the two or three rooms 'going under' without escape.

This is really a major operation, with a good deal of banging and hammering, usually after the guests have departed for the day. A trailer is positioned in the yard outside the kitchen to receive what is hurled out of the bedroom above. Avalanches of rubble cascade past the kitchen, which would be a little disconcerting if we were entertaining the vicar to tea, which we aren't of course.

Then, a heavy cast-iron fireplace is carried downstairs. What a strong man Samson is! The now redundant item is placed in the garage opposite, where it stands alongside other obsolete utensils such as two fridges, an electric cooker, a washing machine and a hoover.

Next to the garage is the stable and tack room, once the home of a spirited hunter or two but now housing the old beds and wooden items no longer in use. There must be a groom writhing in agony, never mind turning, in his grave, to see this lovely old building used solely as a place for storing and chopping wood. After the horses, it was taken over by a family of farm cats, who thought it suited their lifestyle perfectly. However, one by one, they gradually died, only to be exhumed from the rubbish at odd times over the years by an alarmed Evelyn, detailed to do the stable.

By day, Samson and Them make our bedrooms their workplace, exposing large areas of bare wall and subsequently re-clothing them with plaster. It is a salutary experience to sleep in such a room, first removing the old sheet covering the bed. We get used to it and by the end of the day we are often so tired that we hardly notice. Of course, clouds of dust creep towards the front of the house from time to time.

There are a few silver linings. It is amazing how fascinating it is to watch men at work. Better still is to watch men when not at work. With religious regularity, tools are downed every two hours or so; then the builders squat down on some sheet-covered item and open a tin, or bait box as it is called in these parts. Young eyes widen to see what choice morsel might be extracted from within. Reluctantly, I take steps to curb this practice; I feel guilty to see my children salivating whilst the working man eats. Samson and Them do not seem to mind, so eventually I cease to worry. Obviously, their wives overestimate their appetites and an infant often appears clutching a piece of 'foreign' food, like a luminous pink biscuit or a fig roll.

Some mornings, they start earlier than others. At all events, those staying have usually breakfasted by the time the cacophony and clatter begin. One day they arrive whilst I am having the luxury of a long and fragrant bath (during a blissful break between bookings). I can hear an anxious voice downstairs in the kitchen calling after them as they make their way upstairs, 'The wife is in the bath, mind!'

By now I am in fact fully clothed, refreshed and ready to face whatever the day has to offer.

'It's all right, Jimmy,' calls down Samson's mate, 'I'm just scrubbing her back.'

The work goes on. We grin and bear it, but we grin.

Yes, not only is it the season, but it is also the school holidays – a further complication in the improvements saga.

'How *do* you cope with all those children in the school holidays?' they ask.

'Well, of course, we do have a lot of space,' is my usual reply.

These holidays we do not have quite as much space as usual. It is as well the weather is good so that they can play outside which, of course, they are reluctant to do.

They develop a new game called 'Snails'. I pride myself on the inventiveness of my offspring and think little of it. One day, however, whilst in the garden, I stumble across the focal point for this game, the old pram. I casually peer in, only to find that, horror of horrors, it is full of *snails*. It gradually dawns that some sort of competitive mollusc movement is taking place – perhaps even money might be involved?

I resolve to lay on a little more organised recreation. It suits me for I am glad to be out of the house. We have a few mini-trips like this outing to the beach, which is an infantry exercise, the beach being only a field away from the farm. Today, we even have two or three extra boys from up the road; there is therefore quite a crowd going forward, terrifying all wildlife within a radius of about five miles. As usual, the journey is conducted in stages. At the first stop, we play in the river, stripping off rashly in the heat.

'Where have you put your clothes?'

'Over there.'

'Here?'

'Er – I can't remember.'

I can see that we are going to have to have an interesting game of treasure hunts before the afternoon is through. I can imagine the dialogue when Michael and David go home after tea at our house.

'Where are your clothes?' Tones of horror.

'Their mother said we could take them off, and then we couldn't find them.'

Sharp intake of breath: 'You will not be going *there* again.'

The stream, rather sluggish and slow, reaches the sand here and they wade up and down, optimistically waving fishing nets, squealing and squeaking. Meanwhile, a splinter group is playing water rugby with an old can they found embedded in the sand. I told you they were inventive.

'Come on. Come on. We'll go across the beach now.'

We abandon the stream and dunes and race across the flat, unblemished sand – well, fairly unblemished. We still have the fishermen of course, those that are left being considerably better behaved and more friendly, but the relics of former occupancy remain. On an outcrop of tufty dunes in the middle of the sand, known to this family as 'the Island', a wreck is scattered.

'Oh – so that is how you make caravans. . . .'

An odd mattress here, a broken chair there, lie half-buried in the ever-changing sands. This example of pollution and threat to the environment leaves the children cold. They throw themselves into their customary games of racing up and down the dunes and hide and seek (though it is now called something else). I pass. I flop down on a plump sand

137

dune with my plump little daughter and babe and . . . wait. Heads pop up at intervals.

'Have you seen. . .?'

'Which way did he go?'

Great fun! After a seemingly suitable period of time has elapsed, no one has a watch of course, we gird our loins for the final assault – the North Sea itself. It looks so tempting, blue translucence with creamy waves pounding on the firm golden sand. But no matter how warm the weather, these inviting waters hold hidden powers to effect instant freezing. This experience of course does not deter those present today but I restrict their activities (I still have some power) to wave-jumping, which seems to satisfy. Just to be sociable I dabble my own digits in the waves with my daughter from time to time. There is an added hazard at this time of year – jellyfish, for which we keep a weather eye open.

'Right, folks. Ready for the long trek home?'

'Oh no!'

'Can't we stay a bit longer?'

'Oh, it's not fair.'

We are on our way. We reach eventually the stream and I find myself the lucky recipient of sodden sand shoes, shorts, T-shirts, buckets, spades – not to mention a tired toddler, in addition to baby. Aha, here come reinforcements over the horizon; he must have finished sorting the sheep early.

'No – you can't be serious. It can't possibly be five-thirty. . . . I've got the Wotsits' supper to get for seven and I haven't even made the pastry.'

The pace quickens as we head for home but even so, my mind is going much faster than my feet.

What follows is one of life's minor triumphs, which I have to admit I would not have accomplished without the aid of the farmer who transports the extra boys home, baths those of ours who cannot bath themselves and sets the table. Meanwhile the cook hurriedly manufactures flaky pastry and brandy snaps, brings fresh vegetables in from the garden, even irons a tablecloth. Phew – I hope they appreciate it.

They do not. The family we have staying this week is not one of our successes. By and large, my carefully worded photocopied description (code-named 'brochure') discourages all but the dedicated: birdwatchers, walkers, self-contained family party, etc. However, from time to time, someone fails to get the picture. Of course, we occasionally have the 'casual' sent out by the Tourist Board for a night. You can tell the signs: a slight wrinkling of the nose as they cross the threshold, or possibly a 'Where's the nearest pub?' or a 'long way from the shops, aren't you?', a perceptible toss of the head and, 'No, it's not what we're looking for.' Or not even that; they simply disappear. These people are all part of the game, but when you have a family booked in for the week, who have obviously not understood words like 'unsophisticated' or 'bracing', you're in trouble.

You soldier on, imaging that as long as you do your best, your endeavours will conquer all. You try a slightly different tack every night. One night Italian (well, spaghetti), another night health conscious (salad) or, like tonight, comforting family farmhouse fare (steak and kidney pie). But no, half of it still remains on the plates and some slips to the floor. They could have left it on the serving dishes of course but what we have here is a typical 'If I'm paying for this, we're bloody well having it, not leaving it for anyone else.'

The rather meek little wife seems apologetic but she could have scooped up the kids' spaghetti from the floor, couldn't she? But, there again, perhaps she was not allowed. Families, I find, usually clear up after them, only too grateful for having the cooking and washing up done for them. Not these. I can imagine:

'Leave that, Jennifer. Don't touch a thing! Leave it exactly as it is!'

'But, Jeffrey, she'll think. . . .'

'I don't give a damn what she thinks. How she expects us to eat this muck I do not know. Give me fish and chips any day. I mean, she doesn't even supply any ketchup! I ask you!'

You can't please 'em all, I suppose. They are here for the week. They have to make the best of it, and so do we. Never mind, one night we sort them out.

'What's that? Five American students? O.K. We'll fit them in.'

He replaces the phone. 'They're sending five American students down here from the pub.'

'Five? Are you crazy? Where are we going to put them? What sex?'

'Oh, I never asked. Anyway, we'll put them in the two end rooms, three in one and two in the other. Easy.'

Shortly after this rather terse exchange, a brown Escort pulls up and out unfold four enormous young men and one rather small girl. Suddenly, the house is filled with voices and laughter. Huh – well, that'll teach old misery-guts! In the morning our transatlantic friends drink a litre of orange juice and there is an 80 per cent rejection of their ordered English breakfasts.

Meanwhile, outside, the combines are trundling on. Seems a good crop of wheat. Although the actual cutting is done by contractor, the transportation of the stuff up to the silos is undertaken by the resident workforce, which in turn means the loss of a waiter/baby minder on evening stints. However, that's how it goes. He even drives the tractor from time to time, and if that's not keen I don't know what is.

'Where is he tonight?'

'He's driving off the combine, I am afraid. Any excuse, eh!'

However, I am receiving additional help this season. Number One Son prides himself on his sausages. He takes over the grill, leaving the head chef to concentrate her attentions elsewhere.

Now, take a party of four adults (two pairs) and two children (belonging to one pair); add one lovable old spaniel, blind and deaf, and large quantities of alcohol purchased previously for their week's houseparty with us, and you have a surefire recipe for success. The fact that the folk come from London adds the final touch. The children swiftly integrate with ours, each a little astonished at the way the others speak. Hopefully, the London children do not think that our living quarters are permanently covered with sheets and dust.

The Camparis, as we christen them, are here to enjoy themselves. They preface their evening meal with glasses of a pink liquid not popular in these parts. They then proceed to claret which they consume by the box. This artificially induced euphoria certainly has the desired effect on their appreciation of my meals. There are comments like 'Wonderful cook, you married, Mr F.' and 'You surpassed yourself tonight, Mrs F.'

Never mind, they certainly eat every scrap. No rejected items remain on plates or serving dishes (even courgettes!) and, what is more, everything is neatly arranged on the trolley at the end of each meal – so they cannot be that inebriated, can they?

The Camparis have the most wonderful dog. Although deficient in the usual faculties, he soon gets the set-up sorted out with the only remaining sense. He goes up the front stairs with his master, and then, leaving his master, he descends back to ground level by way of the back stairs into the kitchen, which seems to him the best place to be. He quickly 'hoovers' up all the droppings under the table and even intercepts one or two tasty morsels on their way from hand to mouth, much to the consternation of one young dreamer. It is impossible to take exception to this sage old man. The Camparis top their list of perfections by being a family of continental breakfast eaters (rare breeds). We are sorry to see them go.

What have we next?

'What's that? Two couples with two children each? Er – yes. Only two nights? Oh yes. Are you on your way up north for your holidays?' I enquire politely.

Laugh at the other end: 'No, this is our holiday. We're farming folk, too.'

Obviously they are not grain farmers.

''No, we live up in the hills about sixty miles south.'

Not going far either.

Guess who is missing? Guess where he is?

'I know you are "front man" but you have been talking to these folk for at least half an hour, it's really way beyond the call of duty.'

'Well, there is something about farming folk. You can have a proper conversation with them for a start.'

After a prolonged very dry spell, we have a wet Sunday. When I say wet I mean wet. We awake to the cover of cloud rather than the clear blue to which we have become used. By eleven o'clock, just as the farmer is homeward plodding his weary way, the heavens open and by the time he struggles to the haven of the back porch, he is soaked.

'Ah well, that'll put a stop to the combining for a day or so. I thought things were going well.'

It rains on. When my mother arrives for lunch the puddles in the road have combined to produce floods. The children all wanted to play outside, glad of a change from the sunshine. It is a pity that they forgot to put on their jackets and wellies; as they troop back in for lunch there is a certain dampness about them.

'I think you had all better get changed.'

After lunch, the menu for which comprises a choice between sausages and oven chips or left-over vegetarian lasagne, I go riding. No one else wishes to accompany me on this occasion, and my mother regards me over her glasses as if making a note to discuss my certification at her next visit to our family doctor. I look at it like this. If I have taken the trouble to book a ride, the first for ages (for obvious reasons), I go – rain or shine. It certainly is not shining.

The groom does not look quite as cheerful as usual and the horse even less so as we leave the shelter of the stable.

'It's getting lighter over there,' I remark optimistically skywards. I suspect it is an optical illusion as the grey sky is still disgorging its contents down upon us with venom. The horse turns her head towards me and suddenly stops dead. She rests her case. I kick her on; she is only an animal after all, and I daresay her coat will shed water more successfully than mine. As for the groom, she is paid to take out idiots – I mean 'clients' – in all weathers, and on this occasion she is certainly dressed for it. In fact, give her a wide-brimmed hat and she'd be a good candidate for stopping stage coaches. For the time being, the weather is forgotten in my eagerness to catch up on the gossip. There always seems to be plenty in a stable; the odds on horsey relationships staying the course are rather long, and changing stables is frequent and popular. I am so engrossed in all this recent history that I hardly notice the rain until we turn windwards for home. Thereafter, the conversation is punctuated with such questions as:

'Is it going down your neck?'

'Can you see?'

Finally, the stables in sight, she politely enquires as to the water-repellent properties of the red kagool I threw on over my shirt and at my reply that I had thought it was, almost unseats herself. Yes, the phrase 'soaked to the skin' has never had a more authentic foundation, and as I get out of the car at home a large damp pool bears testimony to recent occupancy.

'You must be crackers,' remarks my mother. 'Go and have a bath.'

A quick rub down and the chef's hat is fitted on again. We have an elderly couple staying for the week, Bee, Bee and Ee, and wet or not, they have to be fed. At last, having despatched their meal, we are eating ours (I often receive complaints on the paradox of serving poached salmon in the dining room whilst all that is on offer in the kitchen is baked beans) when the telephone rings. Disjointed phrases from the office can be heard.

'Oh, dear, Jack . . . washed out you say . . . well . . . we'll do our best. . . .'

He returns to the kitchen, his features carefully composed.

'Jack's got a family at the campsite who have been out all day and their tent has been flooded.' He pauses, gathers strength and continues quickly in one breath, 'They're coming here to stay the night.'

'Oh no, how many?'

'A mother, father and six children.'

'Six!' I hear my voice squeak unattractively.

'What could I say? You know what Jack's like? It's the only Christian thing to do. And besides, think of the money!'

Our resident couple for the week are self-contained. They are quietly complimentary about meals and spend their evenings sitting reading. However, they can hardly conceal their curiosity when they see their hosts madly dashing around with mattresses, sheets and blankets, with a great deal of muttering, hopefully unintelligible. No sooner have the diners finished than a frenzied figure rushes in to lay ten places for breakfast. Unfortunately the service has only six settings, and two of the cereal bowls are broken. The shortfall is supplemented by crockery from the Co-op Special Offer run a year or two ago; it bears no resemblance to the existing dining room ware of course but I cannot imagine that 'orphans of the storm' will be too fussy.

Phew, what a game – nearly done – here they are! A charming couple from the West Country, whose temperament and time-clock, I know from experience, will be diametrically opposite to that of North-Easterners. They bring in their stuff and I suddenly find my wellington complement increased a hundred per cent as armfuls of the soggy footwear are thrust apologetically towards me to dry during the night. By now it is 9 pm and the owner of the tent stands cheerfully chatting in the kitchen before he suddenly asks casually, as if it has just crossed his mind: 'Where can we eat tonight? Can you recommend anywhere?'

In rural Northumberland, late on a wet Sunday evening,

even at the height of the tourist season, with half a dozen children, the choice is narrow, to put it mildly. We suggest the pub on the main road.

'Oh, we went there the other night. It was OK but a bit *basic*. We thought we'd try somewhere different. . . .'

Next morning, the elderly couple prudently breakfast early and then, so thoughtfully, spread the 'place settings' round the table so that the overall effect is less cramped. After 'the family' has eaten, the picture is not so much cramped as catastrophic. There is a sea of flotsam, comprising bits of sausages, bacon, egg and other debris, presumably over the white linen of the tablecloth. I know it is under there somewhere.

Mr Camper pays his bill happily and announces that they will be staying at Jack's campsite for the duration so we'll probably see them again, but his final words as he walks through the doorway send chills of horror into the depths of my soul.

'We might come back and stay with you – if the mood takes us!'

In the event, this does not materialise. We only have this hypochondriac friend for two nights and then his extremely charming mama: 'I'm past all that, dear' (the tent).

We now plunge headlong into a week of frantic activity. What had promised to be a peaceful interlude with the elderly couple turns out to be something else. The Tourist Board send down a couple for one night who are exceptionally gregarious and decide to stay another, with evening meal. In the event, they stay for a further seven. Every morning, I make out their bill only to find that they've said to someone 'see you tonight'. I am not complaining. They do excellent PR work, in the absence of the usual exponent. He is busy on the tractor. Another three book in at the same time.

If the harvest is still busy in the field, the garden is not doing too badly either, after all that rain. Every couple of days, I still stagger in laden with courgettes and beans. I am well on the way to the compilation of a not-too-slim volume entitled 'Ways with Courgettes'. There have been some rather rude suggestions in this house, which had better remain unrecorded.

Two-thirds into the harvest and a day of mass exit and entrance in the Bee and Bee department do not combine to produce ideal conditions for a Christening at a distant venue. On the day in question, the prospective godparents and family leave behind a steadily moving combine in the field (with Kevin driving the tractor) and masses of laundry in various stages of process. My brother recently moved to these parts after many years in the Far East. He brings back with him rather more than he had: one Filipino wife, her daughter and one baby son. They have not been UK residents very long before they bring forth the twins to whose spiritual welfare we are about to be entrusted.

The average age of the congregation is probably about eight. Our youngest infant and the twins find the service irksome and preclude all necessity for hymns. We repair with relief to my brother's smart new home. There do seem to be lots of little people, a Malaysian friend bringing her bonny brown babe too. Top quote of the afternoon comes from our four-year-old, who goes round inspecting the prostrate infants closely – as you can do at that age – and in a voice, filled with wonder, concludes: 'Our baby is a different colour from the rest.'

On the subject of twins, it is time for the last of the lambs to be weaned from their mothers. This is not a lengthy business but a noisy one. I am told that the matrons are difficult to deal with, exhibiting exuberant but often erratic behaviour.

I can empathise a little, with the school holidays rapidly speeding to a close. I love having them at home: no packed lunches for some, no frantic juggling of dinner money for others, more relaxed mornings and evenings, the greatest advantage of all probably being that the older ones look after the tinies. However, as the holidays wear on, the house (the back portion of course) does take on the appearance of a massive obstacle course and it might be pleasant to 'see the wood for the trees' – or even a patch of floor, however dirty it might be. Unlike the ewes, I shall have a couple remaining but the relative effect will be equally dramatic.

I do love the Blackfaces. There has been talk of breeding the horns off them. I would campaign most vigorously against such a course. There is nothing like the sight of a horned head or two appearing over the sand dunes – like the vanguard of the cavalry. What is more, they are 'characters' with minds of their own, which may, I suppose, interfere with management but I feel sure gains them the respect of their employer.

We have one wonderful lady, for example, who appears to have three lambs of which it is quite likely that one, possibly two are adopted for reasons which are unclear. She seems dissatisfied with her present living conditions, not to mention her neighbours. Therefore, one sunny morning in late August she gathers her family together and, with what few possessions they have, they set off.

The first hurdle to be negotiated is the vexed barbed wire fence. This does not provide too much of a problem for three agile youngsters but is taken with care by their mama of advancing years; a small sample of woollen coat remains clinging to the fence as a clue to their route. They continue at a fast trot across the next field, one of stubble which is a bit uncomfortable on the old feet and not much to nibble at either. No, she has seen a nice green field on the other side, which looks a likely place. Oh yes – this is more like it. Unfortunately, it seems to be already inhabited by a number of large, shaggy creatures (Galloway crosses) but apart from raising their heads briefly as the family enter the field, they seem little interested.

'We'll spend a few days here,' Mrs Blackie confidentially tells her young. 'Tuck in.'

This pattern of progress is repeated over the week until finally she is very surprised to find herself back where she started. One exciting adventure does occur before this, though. The ewes brought in for sorting have at one point seemed reluctant to do as asked; they make a break just as Mrs Blackie is trotting along the lane on her travels. At the sight of these large and violent-looking strangers, Mrs B. takes off with a kick of her heels, closely followed by babes; true to character the ewes quickly follow at great speed. It so happens that this is the route they are ultimately to take! Perhaps, rather like the decoy hare at the greyhound stadium, something could be fabricated and patented along these lines for just such a contingency?

Ah well – the full circle of life comes round. The pedigree tups are harnessed and marked ready for their meeting with the early lambing ladies.

September

September is the month of endings. Three big sighs of relief –
the end of the harvest, the end of the school holidays and the
end of the bed and breakfast season (to a large extent). On the
other hand, it is the end of summer. . . . Add an extra sigh of
relief this year for the builderwork on the house comes to an
end too. One or two of the little people are very sorry to see
them go, missing the builders and their daily offerings from
the bait box; a piece of confectionary from my tin is simply
not the same. They still have some final touches to the roof
to complete and are to be seen in the autumn sunshine, busy
with binoculars.

'What are you looking for, Samson?'

'Sunbathers on the beach. We saw some once.'

Even though we are enjoying a warm spell – will the good
weather ever end? – I cannot help feeling he is being a little
optimistic here. The sort of tourists who might be found
sunbathing on the beach have gone. I suppose that during
the humdrum round of daily toil, one takes one's diversion
where one can.

Whatever they have been up to outside, a small crack appears
on the ceiling inside the 'guest wing'. A splodge of plaster is
swiftly applied and smoothed over after receipt of this intelligence, with a casual 'anything else?' Anything else? There
are patches of crumbling plaster everywhere – not initiated by
recent builderwork I hasten to add, in larder, dairy, all 'fitted'
cupboards. Round he goes with his shovel of gleaming plaster
cheerfully – it makes a change from chimneys.

The washing machine comes to a halt – again. The engineer is called. 'Over-use,' he declares once more in his tight-

lipped Caledonian tongue. Spoken like a man! What does he mean? It is hardly as if I am getting something for nothing. I must have paid for the wretched thing about five times over with maintenance charges. It runs all day long, especially in summertime, and often half the night too. 'Over-use' . . . well. . . . Anyway, I am glad to have the machine operational again, not to mention anxious to attack the mountain of dirty clothes erupting out of the linen basket. I scoop up an armful and throw it into the hole on my way out of the door on yet another shopping trip. Perhaps I 'overshop' as well.

Some time later, I drive back into the yard with the usual heavily laden car and the younger contingent. As I stagger towards the back door, carrying one cardboard box, I stop still in my tracks and stare uncomprehendingly at a strange sight. There is a puddle of water on the step outside the door, even though the morning is dry. Suddenly, I am joined by Samson and Them, looking rather apprehensive.

'Er, Mrs F, there's been a slight accident. The washing machine must have flooded. When we noticed the water coming under the door, we went in and turned it off.'

'Flooded? But I've only just had it mended.'

'Slight' is not the word. I should have put my feet inside one of those pairs of wellies bobbing around in the porch before I entered. The entire kitchen is under water, which is gradually making its way towards the stairs. Through the window, I catch sight of the face of the hungry farmer returning from his rounds. Ah, I see he has been intercepted by Samson and Them. I wonder what line he will take?

'Something up, love?'

There is no point in prostrating myself on the ground in a hysterical outburst – I would get wet.

'The bleep mechanic could not have replaced the outlet pipe properly!'

Some think it great fun. 'Shall I get our ducks and boats from the bathroom?'

'No you will not. Why don't you sit on the table for a while? Pretend you are shipwrecked.'

Apparently that would do, and with a sigh and several towels, I start on the long process of mopping up, with assistance I may add.

After about half an hour of combined effort, I announce to the world at large that I am going to phone the floor people and order new floor covering. The existing stuff will never be the same again and besides . . . it has been getting me down for some time. After years of floods (minor ones compared with this, it is true) it has flatly refused to remain against the floor at the edges, the curl up the wall becoming more pronounced all the time. Then, there is the smell. No one else seems to detect it, but I can.

Yes, the time has definitely come for replacement. Whilst on the telephone, I decide to call the washing machine people and make my complaint, which I consolidate formally on paper, not expecting for one moment that the fellow will admit the tiniest possibility of liability.

After the interlude in the office, fired with fresh zeal I return to the mopping and at last, by the time the older children return from school, the job is done.

'Hello, why is the floor wet?'

'Have you had another flood?'

'Why are the wellies wet?'

On Saturday, we have a walk round the farm 'en famille'. This is a rare occurrence these days for obvious reasons. The pace is rather slow and I carry one on my front and he carries one on his back. It is a long walk for short legs and various sights have to be pointed out when interest and energy flag.

We follow the stream for a while and each small bridge has to be stood upon – some are pretty crumbly and unused – to inspect the waters for fish. Then, land, water and sky are scoured for interesting specimens of wild life in general. We do have budding naturalists in our midsts. Today we see five kingfishers, a golden eagle, half a dozen pine martens, four reindeer. . . .

Actually, when you walk the fields quietly alone, you often

151

see the odd rare bird, which has to be identified in the book when you get home. The sight of heron, fox or deer is almost commonplace, but always a breathtaking delight. Here are Mr and Mrs Swan gliding round the bend with their family, which this year is almost as big as ours.

We proceed to tracking exercises, trying to identify prints on the earth, or better still, on the beach. This always gives enormous scope for the mind of the imaginative naturalist.

Unfortunately the dog accompanying us today does not like children. In fact, he does not like anyone much and will not even allow the boss to touch him unless he is ill or hurt. On occasions like today he hovers just within earshot. He does have a certain notoriety – a very bad habit in fact – in that within the confines of the sheep pens, if asked to work, he will sink his teeth into any leg which hoves into view. In this he does give some deference to the boss, but this habit makes him unpopular with the staff (Kevin) and various relatives who turn up periodically to help sort sheep.

We are reliably informed that he is a Good Dog and this side of his character is due solely to excitement, not malice, but this is little comfort to someone lying on the ground writhing in agony, minus several ounces of fabric and flesh.

The only other problem with this dog is his heart. Apparently, he has some sort of congenital defect in this area, discovered cleverly by the vet, who subsequently advised that outings in extremes of cold and heat were contra-indicated.

Today he is on good form. The weather is typically autumnal with little wind and an unmistakable blurring in the outline of the hills. At each command, prior to execution, he does a sort of ritualistic dance three times round his tail. His audience, with one exception, finds it highly entertaining and claps enthusiastically.

On our way homewards we stop for a few moments to chat to the current holiday cottage occupants, clad in their thermal underwear, draped over the gate. Strains of Mozart are faintly audible from within and I cannot help noticing one or two discarded champagne bottles protruding from the dustbin. Oh yes – we have all sorts.

He is a most extraordinary man who can be seen, striding over the sand dunes, his long black mackintosh billowing in the wind, his epaulettes etched against the sky. Not a birdwatcher or even a rambler this one: simply here to escape from phone and fax and . . . things. His companion, not his wife as he is always at pains to point out, is a rather glamorous young woman, thermal underwear or not. They always come in autumn. They are from another world.

Meanwhile, the combine is moving on relentlessly towards the moment when it stops for another year. No matter how mechanised or subcontracted this side of farming has become, there is a huge lifting of burden from shoulders when all is safely gathered in. Not that there seems even a moment to stand still and savour the satisfaction. No, trailer loads of wheat rumble up to the silo every day until all has gone.

Oh happiness – there is more than he thought. He is not by nature a pessimist so therefore his estimates of the mountains in the shed must simply have been inaccurate, gloriously so. He seems to find it quite fun crawling slowly up the road carting the valuable cargo, not that the price is up to much, but that's another story. On his final trip, he manages to fall foul of some pointed items on the road, producing a puncture – imagine the irony, the frustration. Fortunately, he is offered a lift by a sympathetic fellow farmer to the village from where he has to call out tyre services in the town to come out and assist. This all takes *time* and detracts from that moment of triumph when all is despatched.

That out of the way, we can turn to the vexed question of straw. What has to be baled is quickly baled, some in huge fat rolls, others in smaller, rectangular blocks.

In the first year of our marriage, I remember spending an extremely painful couple of days assisting in the stacking of these latter items. Not only were they heavy but the string cut into my soft, lily white hands. Tearful, I was determined not to give up. Since that time, the only other contact I have made with bales of any kind has been to sever the string and kick to cattle wintering indoors, and I have not done that for a while. At this point, the lip of any reader who happens to be a farmer's wife may curl.

What is not baled is burned. This is a matter of controversy these days because of pollution – not to mention road and rail visibility – but guess who loves it? Off he goes after lunch, a box of matches in his pocket and a gleam in his eye. Hours later, he returns exhausted, smelling of smoke and covered in smuts. It has been a successful burn, apparently.

So much for the fire. Back to the flood. Naturally, the engineer denies all knowledge of the incident so I approach my local NFU Mutual man. Stanley is an utterly charming gentleman, and I choose the words with care. He even rises at the entrance and departure of a lady. He is polite, even laughing at his client's jokes. He himself tells rather bad jokes which I understand improve in the sole company of his own sex, or perhaps it is merely a case of the liquid unleashing of inhibitions? However, by day or by night, he articulates slowly and precisely, rather like Brian Redhead, and his apparel is always immaculate. The picture he presents therefore is a striking contrast to his clients but he seems quite undaunted by this discrepancy.

He is in a good mood today, recently returned from a brief trip to the Mediterranean. Not only is he eager to share tales of sun and sea, but to my horrified astonishment he suddenly announces that he is going to do something very rude. Before I can gather my young and flee, he whips undone the buttons on his shirt and exposes a deeply suntanned chest, rather a lot of it. I decide the moment has arrived to steer him back to the topic in hand, which I readily agree is nowhere near as interesting as the Mediterranean, but the result of which will hopefully defray the large expenditure incurred with the purchase of new floor covering for the kitchen. It will, of course, *take time*. Forms are completed. Cups of tea are consumed.

In the meantime, the fitter and his mate arrive to do the necessary. I have decided to be completely frivolous and order a new bedroom carpet too. This will mean that for six months of the year we can sink our toes into the luxury of silky pile, leaving it to be enjoyed by the Bee and Bees over the remaining period.

The fitter is not a cheerful man, his mate is even less so. They look far from delighted at the task before them. The fitter accompanies me round the rooms to be 'transformed', his face growing longer every second. At last, he stands before the huge, heavy wardrobe in our bedroom and shakes his head; it is not in his brief to move furniture anyway, or something to that effect – but this particular piece is ridiculous. Still muttering under his breath, he returns to the kitchen to commence operations there. They unpack their tools in sulky silence whilst Evelyn and I heave what furniture we can out of their way. Evelyn's expression is eloquent. Finally, they begin work with reluctance.

At this point, the head of the household comes in. A quick assessment of the situation produces the decision to lunch out. Before our departure, however, we consider the vexed question of the wardrobe. He brings out his all-purpose penknife and after a few moments of manipulation, we move the large pieces of this admittedly cumbersome cupboard from the room. As we walk out of the kitchen where the fitter and his mate are toiling in silence, it is irresistible: 'The wife and I have just moved the wardrobe for you, son.'

The fitter looks quite surprised.

Once this job is finished, Evelyn and I begin the big job of putting our house back in order. We have a three-part plan:

1. Clearing up after the builderwork.
2. Moving downwards and outwards, i.e. the opposite of what we did in the spring.
3. Sorting out the kitchens and bedrooms after the laying of the new flooring and (ambitious this) chopping up the old bedroom carpet and bits of new stuff to fit little bedrooms.

All this takes *time* but once it is completed, we can stand back and admire the improvements as an overall effect. The areas of grey virgin plaster upstairs do not look particularly pretty but we are glad we no longer have to position heavy objects against the wall in places in order to keep them up – or prevent plaster from falling out in chunks. Neither do we have to worry about toddlers disappearing up old unused chimneys.

Another piece of good news is the igniting of our old friend, the Aga, for the winter. However, this is not quite as straightforward as it sounds, as it entails the presence of Bert, the boiler expert. Now, lurking in our garage and back kitchen in a variety of large boxes for the best part of a year has been a new central heating system, which Bert confidently predicts will be the answer to all our problems. After phone conversations and ansaphone messages at intervals over the period since its arrival, Bert decides that, when he comes out to clear out the Aga, he will make a start.

The fact that it is about 6 pm does not deter Bert, who is not a nine-to-five man. Problem number one is removal of the old boiler, which is in fact all that he does at the first session, so to speak. There is a great deal of grunting and groaning and complaints about how he is sweating (a phenomenon which does not occur too often one suspects) but at last, the ugly old apparatus is removed, leaving Bert looking like Lennie Henry on an off day, but triumphant none the less.

Over the following few days, the fitting up of the new boiler is undertaken amid the usual monologues about his health, that of his ever-increasing family, and the dreadful state of the world in general. He gives me a complete run-down on his gardening year too.

'Onions is bad. I usually have enough onions to last till Easter; I doubt if I'll last till Christmas this year. . . .'

'I tried growing Jerusalem artichokes this year. I was telling whatsisname's wife, you know him that lives up by what-do-you-call-it; anyway, I was telling her and she comes out with "Artichokes? You mean Fartichokes?" "Oh, no," I said, "what with that beer they give you nowadays – if you see something going past your window at about a hundred miles an hour, don't worry, it'll be me!" '

He continues with mutterings about how everything has changed in the boiler world. He works away, injected intermittently with essential infusions of tea, and the new boiler gradually begins to take shape.

'They're like bloody Christmas trees, these damned things,' he grumbles at one stage. I pause to be enlightened on this analogy.

'All them bits and pieces you have to put on them,' he concludes. Ah.

Finally, we have a more efficient central heating system and the Aga emanates its winter warmth. Gosh, the house is uncharacteristically warm. Have to open a window or two!

Now we have spread ourselves out again, this does not mean that we cannot still receive visitors. With the two spare bedrooms, we can still manage three to five – instead of the eight or nine we sometimes squeezed in during the summer. However, we are on our last booking now, although there may still be the odd casual during the month if the weather remains good.

Madeline and Tom have been coming here for years, sometimes with Mother and sometimes without. On this occasion, Tom and Madeline are alone – well, except for Spot, their spaniel. If there were to be an award given to the softest dog on earth, Spot would surely have all the other competitors cowering in submission. When he returns from his day out, we have to lock up the little ones before he will cross the threshold because he is terrified of them. Once in the house, if he hears their approach he hides beneath a chair or behind Madeline, quaking. Spot is used to a quiet life.

If Spot were to receive such an award, then Madeline and Tom (with or without Mama) would be sure contenders for the award of the Best Guests. They eat their meals with speed and precision, leaving no trace on my pristine white linen. The china is always neatly stacked on the trolley, waiting simply to be wheeled into the kitchen, and their plates are always clean. They move quietly around the house, do not commandeer the bathroom, are always up on time, show an interest in the children. In fact they even entertain one or two for long periods – a practice I should not really encourage but I am so grateful. . . .

All this is topped off with a super sense of humour. Yes, you can have a relaxing chat and a laugh with them from time to time, without having to back off, shift from foot to foot, worrying about what is in the oven. They are perfect.

We do have some regulars who have to be hidden from in order to get anything done. There they are lurking at the bottom of the stairs before breakfast, waiting for a pre-prandial chat; you carry the meal in (if it ever gets cooked) and it congeals and cools, even on the heated tray, by the time they have given you their itinerary for the coming day.

After breakfast, you lie low whilst they patter backwards and forwards to their rooms for things forgotten before they finally board the car. It is not until you hear third gear going into the distance that you know it is quite safe to come out from the cupboard under the stairs to clear the table. As five or six pm draws near, you begin to become decidedly twitchy, waiting for the rusty hinges of the front door to herald their return and the whole process beginning again. It is in times like these that you keep a picture of the cheque to be received at the end of the week firmly implanted in your mind.

I see a contorted face at the kitchen window as I am putting an array of cereal packets on the table for the children's breakfast. Who on earth can it be? It is Madeline back from taking Spot for his early morning walk.

'What on earth is the matter? Come in! You look dreadful.'

'It's Spot. He has killed a hen!'

'Oh – is that all?' I am amazed at this temerity but I suppose breeding will out in the end, as they say. I laugh.

'All? It's no laughing matter.' Madeline collapses on to a chair, probably already embellished with Weetabix, but she seems impervious to such detail. She pulls a large handker-chief from her pocket and dabs her eyes.

'Where is he?' I enquire with interest.

'Oh – I've put him in the car and told him what a naughty boy he is.'

'Don't worry. It doesn't really matter. We've plenty more. . . . It's only natural for dogs to chase hens. . . .'

This is something townsfolk simply do not understand. Animals kill each other. Their mortality cannot be compared with that of humans. Life is cheap and, no matter what propaganda is put out in many a children's book, they often kill for the sheer hell of it, not necessarily to eat or to defend themselves.

Living on a farm, you learn a lot about life and death. On the other hand, one does become a little peeved when seven or eight hundred pounds worth of cow drops down dead, reducing its value to a fiver from the knackerman if you are lucky – but hens, well. . . .

Here he comes, his entrance as usual carefully timed as closely as possible to coincide with the arrival of the school bus and his bacon and eggs. On hearing Madeline's story, he comforts her with the words, 'Don't worry! You'll get it for your supper tonight. We waste nothing here. *And* no eggs for your breakfast this morning!'

'I never want to see an egg again,' wails Madeline, her sense of humour having died with the hen.

On one of Spot's evening excursions, Madeline comes in excitedly to report some errant gentlemen amassed on the road. Investigation reveals that the lads concerned are en route to the ladies up the lane for a spot of slap and tickle. Oh no, we all know what this means (again)! It means there will be a steady stream of progeny, starting with the pedigrees in January, right through to the main population explosion in March.

Ah well, not much we can do about it now. I daresay that there may be a morning-after pill for sheep but as there is some doubt as to how long this particular exercise has been going on and which ladies have been participating, it is hardly worth contemplating – and as they are expected to submit shortly anyway, it could cause some problems both hormonal and mental I should imagine.

'I don't know what he's playing at. I think he is going off his head. I wish he'd make up his mind. Does he want us pregnant or not?'

During Tom and Madeline's stay, we have two beautiful young ladies from London visit for a couple of nights. We do not really discover why. Their presence has a dramatic effect on Tom, though. I have never known them linger so long over breakfast; gales of female laughter come forth from the dining room, punctuated by the odd tinkle of a teaspoon. Tom must be drawing deep on his vast fund of anecdotes this morning.

The young ladies have a tale to tell too. They appear to be anxious to take in as many quaint experiences as possible, whilst 'out in the wilds'. Therefore, instead of staying in for a staid meal in the farmhouse, they elect a night out on the town.

To begin with, they have a few jars at the local wine bar, where anyone over the age of twenty is regarded with suspicion, thereafter repairing to the Indian restaurant. The room seems to be crowded with rather irate patrons and the intelligence is soon received that the chef and his assistant have had the misfortune to be involved in a car accident and are currently grateful for refreshment and hospitality from the NHS. Therefore, the poor manager, indoctrinated with the old adage that the show must go on, is performing at the stove himself, single-handed. When he realises his limitations, he proceeds to lock the doors, and thus the establishment, renowned for its late-night culinary output, has the key turned at the unearthly hour of ten.

On account of his one-man show there are naturally a few delays here and there, and there are some rumblings of discontent amongst those fortunate enough to be allowed to dine. Of course, our London lovelies lap all this up, enjoying every minute. When at last they reluctantly feel they should depart, there is no one else in sight. The doors are very securely locked, they cannot escape. This is the stuff! If you want a straight-forward, well-produced Indian meal, served with speed, there are probably thousands of such places in London, but this: this is style. This is probably the reason I like Londoners – you can get away with an awful lot in the interests of eccentricity.

I have come to a decision. I have had enough of hens. They are simply no longer playing the game. Some are not laying at all; those who are seem to be taking such a pride in hiding the eggs. Therefore, their days are numbered. The round has been dismantled, owing to non-reliability. Any eggs discovered during the hens' period on death row are either eaten or given away. Why are we waiting? Well, the prospect of spending an afternoon wringing the necks of forty-five or so hens, extremely active and devious birds at that, is not an attractive one.

During this period of 'borrowed time' the ladies seem to lay in all sorts of odd places. One chooses the welly box in the back porch, which at least means it is being used for something. The outside door is locked until we get up and go out, which is reasonably early most days. However, on Sunday mornings things are a little more relaxed, we can occasionally lie in bed even as late as 8 am by which time the welly box layer is outraged. When I descend the stairs into the wonderfully warm kitchen, I can hear a funny noise. I am used to the throb of the new boiler now, and it is not a child's noise; it is not even the squeak of a mouse. No, it is the beak of an angry bird against the window pane. I look at her. She looks at me. I know the feeling. I open the door and she gratefully sinks into her chosen nest. Another, even sillier bird, chooses the old go-kart in the garage. . . .

I suddenly realise the weekly outing laden with new-laid eggs was my only social life, and now I have lost it. Oh well – too late to worry about that now.

Kevin has been given the job of executioner, and he does

not like hens. Over the years it has fallen largely his lot to clean out the hen house from time to time and the experience does tend to lead you into a genuine antipathy to the creatures. However, even Kevin feels quite sorry for the final few. Hens must have some feelings and watching one's friends bite the dust in quick succession, knowing that your turn will follow, might be a little distressing. At the end of the day, we are left with Jack's bantams, two cockerels and a few of the old order who hopefully will continue to supply our table, when they feel like it.

One advantage is that I should have less interference in the garden. It would be just my luck to have retained the star culprits. At all events, back to the garden I must go. All summer it has not really been a success. It is true to say that I have had some fruit and vegetables, and would have had more had it not been for certain members of the cow family, but the flower beds have been badly affected by drought and bugs and my lettuces and spinach floundered early on, much to the relief of some. As usual, the area has not been touched for ages, except to harvest what there was.

As we proceed through autumn, we have the odd rainy day, and when I finally get round to close scrutiny I find that not only are the weeds beginning to flourish again but also annuals given up for lost have sprung to life, and others have self-seeded. Oh dear, there is a lot of work to be done here. It is a case of the autumn attack, as opposed to the spring surge. The only consolation is that there is not quite the same urgency as there is little planting to do; we are winding down rather than winding up. However, I must get to work as I know from bitter experience that I will lose the garden if I do not catch it now.

So once again, where shall I begin? I decide on the flower beds as, once they are cleared, I should like to put in a few wallflowers, bulbs, etc., for next spring.

My goodness, here is that little gem I gleaned from Josephine's garden when they moved house. She was an 'egg person' who very kindly gave me a good deal, but my poor husbandry and our unsuitable conditions caused the demise of most. This delicate little shrub actually survived, and it was a pity no one saw its exquisite flower when it was totally overpowered by greenfly-covered marigolds. Never mind, there is always next year.

Out come the straggling sweet peas, which were never up to much. Barrow after barrow of weeds are breathlessly led out of the garden. Oh yes, large tracts of good crumbly earth are appearing and, do you know, that garden which one of the children planted with his single packet of seeds is still there. Not only there but thriving. After the weeds are removed it becomes a riot of colour and bloom. It must be true that some of us have green fingers and some do not. Perhaps in a few years' time, he can take over the management of the entire plot, but as he is only six years old I suppose it would be unwise to saddle him with such an undertaking too early. He is full of bright ideas, though.

'I wish we could plant ice lolly sticks,' he declares wistfully one day, extracting the last luscious lick from a particularly succulent specimen. 'Then, when they grew into trees, we could just pick one whenever we wanted.' He understands the principles of life all right.

Meanwhile, out in the fields, the sowing is well underway. There is no time for rest.

'Is he in?'

'Er, well, he is in the bath. Is there anything I can do Jack?'

Chuckle: 'Well, you can tell him to get a towel round his body pretty fast and get along here as his heifers are in the garden.'

'Oh dear.'

I hardly dare disturb him. He looks so comfortable, immersed in warm soapy suds with the latest Desmond Bagley but, after all, they are his cows and we all know what cows do to a garden. They cannot have done too much damage yet as Jack still has hold of his sense of humour.

*   *   *

Next, we have a visit from the law. Here he is sitting comfortably in the kitchen, his good-natured features wrapped round a mug of tea, his machine emanating the usual unintelligible racket. The reason for his visit tonight is to warn us that there is some sheep stealing in the district. We ourselves mislaid half a dozen this time last year, it must be the season.

We cover the subject at some length and then move on to the fascinating topic of the recent influx of 'foreigners' in the area. One of our farm cottages is currently rented by a young couple who used to come to the holiday cottage and 'fell in love' with the place; they have given up their jobs and security in the city and are enjoying a better quality of life and writing creative stuff.

There are other erstwhile holiday cottage habituées from another city in another nearby house, a group of feminists, regarded *very* suspiciously round here as you can imagine. On top of this, some tumbledown cottages belonging to our landlord have been put on the market, the advertisement saying 'derelict'. I know a little estate-agent speak from the inside and understand phrases like 'scope for modernisation' and 'quaintly rustic'. I simply cannot believe that these two piles of rubble are what is on offer. Never mind. In the short period between the date of advertising and the date of closure, literally dozens of interested parties descend upon the quiet, clean-living backwater of Goswick. We, who never see a soul other than the odd native, gradually get used to the stream of cars.

'It is getting to the stage,' declares P.C. Jones with confidence as he regards my daughter's expensive third birthday present, 'when, if you slapped a "For Sale" notice on that Wendy House and put it outside, they would come rushing down here in droves.'

We laugh but we all share a feeling of vague discomfort. We know all about winds here on the bleak Northumbrian coast – but the Wind of Change is an unfamiliar one.

Dipping Time again. 'Oh look, my rubber trousers have

split!' the cry goes up.

'You'll just have to wear your swimming trunks.'

In the event, he wears the split trousers and gets Kevin to do all the work, which is standard practice, so I don't know why he was worried about the rubber trousers at all.

Outside, the sheep have their say:

'Oh, Lord, here he comes again, looking One of those Magnificent Men in their Flying Machines in that ridiculous helmet and those flapping trousers. What a sight! Kevin doesn't look much better, but we all know who will be doing all the work. What a pong!' I'll swear it gets worse every year. What do they put into it? I suppose it's better than getting the dreaded scab.'

'Oh-oh – here comes the Snapper. I do wish he wouldn't get so excited. One of these days he'll drop down dead with excitement. A dog did that on my last farm; there we all were one day, being – er – ushered into the farmyard and he was dashing backwards and forwards barking and snapping and then, suddenly, he went down, dead as a stone. The farmer was quite upset. Blamed one of us for butting him or something. It was a shock anyway. Hello – our turn – here we go. Damn – I've forgotten my nose clip. Still I'll be able to hold my breath for the short time he expects you to be in. Ha – I'm not complaining. Bye. Whoosh!'

'What on earth does this mean?' I stare uncomprehending at the piece of paper. 'One tup, eighty Blackfaces, eighty Mules . . . I'm sorry; I don't understand. I thought you went to market today to *sell* a tup?'

'Well, this is it. I didn't sell the creature as trade was so bad, so I bought some instead. It would have been madness not to.'

I wonder if that nice Mr McTavish at the Bank will share this interesting line of thought?

We say goodbye to Tom and Madeline, sorry to see them go. On the other hand, we are glad to receive their big fat cheque. We are also glad to have the house to ourselves. This must convey itself telepathically, for Madeline says suddenly, 'You'll be glad to see the back of us. The minute that door closes, you'll be up those stairs, stripping off. . . .'

'Eh? What do you mean? Surely you don't think . . .?'

'The sheets I mean, you daft cow.'

Yes, we have got to know each other quite well over the years.

The house is ours for a few days. Then suddenly a wizened face appears at the kitchen window.

'Do you do bed and breakfast, love?'

'Er, yes.'

'Could you manage three of us for tonight, love?'

Here we go again. Luckily, Evelyn made up the beds. I think I have removed some of the pillows. I really must buy some more before next season. We have approximately sixteen beds in this house but only possess twelve pillows. Therefore, if we have more than four guests, guess who has to do without?

I duly direct my not-very-welcome guests round to the front door. This gives me the much needed few minutes to spray polish into the air and repossess the necessary pillows. Whoops, I have forgotten towels. Too late. They are coming in at the front door.

'You'll do us an evening meal, won't you, dear? We don't want to go out again.'

'I – er.' It is already 5.30 pm.

'Thank you, love. Now, which way is it?'

Now, it seems that husband and wife are not in accord over their social arrangements, as he mutters to me in an aside whilst mounting the stairs something about being all right for a few jars down at the nineteenth hole. I have my doubts but smile brightly.

Whilst the party is upstairs unpacking, the Bee and Bee TV is swiftly unplugged from the kitchen and hurtled through the house, teetering dangerously on the corners, pell mell for the guests' sitting room. Fresh in from feeding the dogs, the poor worker is turned round on the step and despatched to the stable to chop wood for the fire, the visible evidence of our hospitality. Meanwhile, guess who is frantically ironing a tablecloth, which has been reposing lazily in the basket, where it would probably have remained for weeks.

Soon, all is ready. I have prepared a meal out of nothing. It is not quite a silk purse but . . . it will do.

Afterwards, the male member of the team ambles through to the kitchen to ask the cost. What follows is what can only be described as a misunderstanding. He thinks he can get Bee, Bee and Ee for the price of Bee and Bee, and is a little upset. Nonetheless he pays, and nonetheless they still all troop off to the nineteenth for a few jars.

Next morning, I come downstairs before seven and am greeted with, 'I shall have to report you to the Tourist Board, love.'

'Eh? Why?'

'Them beds. I haven't slept a wink all night, and then why is your water brown? I am making a cup of tea. Luckily we brought some water with us. Then, there is your prices, dear. Ridiculous.'

The water was cut off yesterday.

'But look here, it is in the leaflet,' I protest weakly as I dash off to consult the document in question.

They make a very large breakfast, denude the fruit bowl, decorate the tablecloth and depart.

I am glad the season is over.

October

'We plough the fields and scatter the good seed on the land. . . .' I do enjoy a Harvest Festival. Something takes me back down the years, the smell of the fruit and vegetables stacked on the tables in gleaming piles, or the jars of chutney and pickles – not donated by this mother, I regret to say. Never mind, here we are, Evelyn and I, on the usual uncomfortable wooden seats with all the other fond mothers, watching their little dears singing the familiar harvest hymns with such enthusiasm. You can always pick out our children, the ones with the holes in the knees of their trousers or garments back to front or inside out. The absolutely 100 per cent fool proof test is toothpaste round the mouth and halfway down the jumper.

Anyway, on this occasion, the top class is performing an ambitious little piece depicting a bright little lad buying a loaf of bread and following it backwards to its origins. I suspect that this might come as a bit of an eye-opener to one or two who probably thought that it was dug out of the soil ready-sliced in its neat polythene bag. My children have at least had the experience of watching their parent kneading life into dough on the kitchen table. At all events for this imaginative little play, full marks must be given to the teacher of the first class, full of creativity and artistic ideas.

Hello, they are about to perform something else after another little hymn. In a brief summary we are told that it concerns the movement of the combine through the ears of corn. It is great fun for the combine but not a lot for the others, and I am glad they briefed us first – I would never have guessed.

At last it is all over and we all file out of the building

slowly, the parents making more noise than the children. Evelyn and I exchange glances. Because we are not villagers, we tend to feel 'left out in the cold' on such occasions (a silly metaphor as it is usually far too stiflingly hot) but we glean snippets of background information one way and another – and piece it together in the car on the way home like a jigsaw puzzle.

Here I am playing the game of 'Guessing the Occupation' again. I really don't feel I have become much more expert at it over the years: 'poets' have turned out to be computer programmers; a 'clerk' once turned out to be the curator of a natural history museum. . . . I am wrong again; I was quite certain that Mr Peart was in the Regular Army, given his rather short-cropped hairstyle, somewhat hearty manner and quiet, subservient wife.

Would you believe it, at the end of the week I discover he is a quality controller of a rather superior small brewery. With very little encouragement, he will launch himself into a long discourse concerning the manufacture of this excellent beverage, indulging in lateral philosophy on human behaviour in general from time to time. In short, Mr Peart is a very interesting gentleman who is discussing a subject very dear to our hearts which has more to it than meets the eye. Mr Peart, for his part, is very interested in varieties of barley grown and the reasons involved in such choices. Therefore, we find that not only do we conduct interesting conversations with our 'clients' but occasionally, there may be mutual advantage. In order to substantiate his points, Mr Peart has even gone to the extreme of presenting us with samples of his product. We do not have many visitors like Mr Peart.

Number One Son is very helpful when it comes to cleaning out the cottage. He is helpful at any time, as long as there is sufficient financial inducement. On Saturday mornings his mother is only too pleased to meet his requirements in this respect, as speed is the essence. However, on this particular occasion he has had the nerve to go off to a friend's house for the weekend. Therefore, I take his immediate inferior in the pecking order, whose sense of responsibility is lacking, plus a four-year-old to keep an eye on, as his petition to accompany us was too vocal to refuse. Fortunately, the cottage does not need a great deal of attention; it is spotless in fact. However, at this time of year the fires have to be lit upstairs and down, thereafter it is simply a matter of changing the bed linen.

After my initial assessment I leave them to their own devices as work is easier without their 'help'. I realise my mistake when I hear the words, 'Come on, you can get out on to the roof through this window,' followed by silence. The pair are subsequently detailed to ground-floor activities like checking the inventory where surely they can't do much damage. Co-ordination is not Number Two Son's forte – what is? The simplest task seems beyond his capabilities. However, this morning he exceeds his personal best by dropping a glass jug from a height of several feet on to a tray of newly acquired glasses. 'Whoops!' he exclaims with optimism.

Meanwhile, back at the ranch, there seems to be a good deal of euphoria around. I rack my brains for the cause. Ah yes, the sowing is finished. As we now have all winter corn, this does represent something of an achievement. At last, a sigh of relief and a point at which to sit back and relax maybe? Fat chance! When I think of the simplistic theories I used to hold on growth: sowing, weeding, watering, harvesting. Nothing is simple now it seems. No, the tiny ear of corn is cosseted in every way over the next nine months or so. No room for the free thinker or development of character. He is subjected to a variety of treatments, pampered to protect him from all ills. . . . For the moment, however, the farmer turns his attention to other areas.

'Daddy has bought another funny sheep.'

This particular purchase turns out to be a Blue-Headed Leicester. It does seem ironic that lively, attractive ladies like 'The Blackies' should have to be introduced to such ugly creatures:

> *'Have you seen who he's brought home for us this time, girls?'*
>
> *'Not another of those big-nosed guys?'*
>
> *'Big-nosed? Let's put it this way, if it were much bigger he'd be in serious danger of not being able to see what he was doing.'*
>
> *'I suppose we could always run away.'*
>
> *'Look, dear. I have learned over a period of years that when you are left in the field with these gentlemen, the best thing you can do is to sidle up to the nearest one to you and get it over with as soon as possible. That way, you have a chance of being left in peace thereafter. Otherwise, you have the brutes sniffing round you for ever. . . .'*
>
> *'You are probably right. I suppose it is just a case of closing your eyes and thinking of Scotland. . . .'*
>
> *'In any case, it isn't our immediate problem. The others always go first. Let's just relax – eat grass whilst the sun is shining.'*

'What are you doing this afternoon, dear?'

'The tups' feet.'

Yes, before their introduction to the ladies of the farm, the gentlemen have to have a good going-over, I mean image assessment. Today they are having a complete manicure – or is it pedicure?

> *'Here we go again, mate. We'll end up looking like My Little Pony if we're not careful. If he comes across with the curling tongs I'm off.'*

He does not. The very large gentleman previously described, however, is not even keen on having his feet done. He stares in mute disbelief at the 'scissors' and bends his great head. The 'beautician' is not very happy about continuing the attempt at improvement in appearance although, Heaven knows, he could do with some help. The operator has the uncomfortable feeling, somewhere just below his middle actually, a sort of prickling sensation inside, a premonition you might call it – that discretion might be the better part of valour here. He throws down his sword and his opponent retreats. His toe nails did not look too bad anyway.

'Naow.' My daughter flatly refuses to push her foot any further into her welly, her huge brown eyes filling with tears. These eyes will melt many hearts before she is through. Tears begin to trickle slowly down her face. Now, had it been her elder brother, we would all be wearing welly boots by now as he has the unique facility of being able to activate his tear ducts in the same way that a cow might let down her milk when she has been kept waiting for half an hour. It is pretty sensational; I sometimes wish I could do it myself.

Meanwhile, it is plain that however hard I push, the foot simply will not go in. I cannot understand it, her feet cannot have grown an inch since yesterday. With a sigh, I remove the leg completely and put my hand inside the unyielding footpiece. Oh, no wonder there was no room for the foot – there is a large plastic pig inside the toe. Plastic cows, plastic pigs, sheep, hens, ducks – we have them all. They stand shoulder to shoulder on the floor with alligator and hippo, dinosaurs and ducks – and so the tapestry is thrown open wide.

In the corner of the kitchen late at night, something moves. It is not the quick flash of a mouse, although that is bad enough. It is definitely a jump. Oh dear it is that time of year again, it is a frog. Inevitably, in autumn we have an invasion of tiny frogs which all inmates of this house, with one exception, find absolutely fascinating. Unlike mice, you do have to respect frogs. I know that. They eat grubs and enemies in the garden – and for this I really am grateful. I just wish they wouldn't come in the house, I am terrified of cold-blooded creatures large and small. I would rather walk through a field of cows with newborn calves, with a few Aberdeen Angus bulls thrown in, than a field of frogs. We all have our hang-ups I suppose.

It goes without saying that family outings do not occur

very often. The logistics are simply too complex to contemplate. When we purchased our last car, some years ago, my mother made muted suggestions about a mini-bus. But no, in common with many farming and non-farming families in this area we possess a Volvo Estate. It is now rather battered but unbowed and not only is it amazing the number of children it can carry but it can easily absorb a week's shopping too. Another attribute of this old vehicle is its supremacy on the road. You find few vehicles will fight with a battered old Volvo.

Anyway, today we are all assembled in the family car for an unprecedented trip into the hills. A little guilt is felt as you have the sneaking suspicion that the younger children at least must imagine that the whole world is composed of flat plains with few trees or inhabitants. On this scenic tour, the gasps and exclamations at the change in scenery are out of all proportion for a thirty-mile run inland. One last bend – one or two faces are just beginning to look green – and we are here. A tiny village nestling in a hollow in the heart of the Cheviots hosting the last of the Shepherds' Shows. It is well-attended, the normal population increased several thousandfold.

Where have they all come from? The air is heavy with hot dogs and loud fairground music. The children cannot believe their eyes. We hastily disembark, leaving 'Daddy' to dispose of the car as best he can and, holding firmly to a baby and a couple of tiny hands, welly-booted we advance into the thick of things.

'Can I go on the dodgem cars/roundabout/rifle range?' come the cries of those in the vanguard and you soon find yourself digging deep into pockets.

'What's that pink stuff those people are eating?'

'Can I have some?'

'Can I have some joke spectacles?'

After about half an hour of walking round the fairground, the phrase 'soaking up the atmosphere' takes on full meaning. It seems that no sense has been left unimpaired. Your eyes are smarting with smoke unspecified, your ears are ringing with the clamour mingled with 'music', your nose seems to be totally filled with cooking and diesel oil, your arms and legs are aching with the carrying and clinging to infants.

You tell yourself that this is not what you came for. You came to see the traditional arts of arm wrestling and stick-dressing, the making of Northumbrian pipes – but quite honestly, you need a drink. There seem to be quite a number of gentlemen on the ground who have had similar thoughts and have obviously given little pause between thought and deed.

We make our way towards the house which has recently been purchased by friends – it is thanks to their invitation that we are here at all. The door opens and we suddenly find ourselves amid familiar faces and warm hospitality. Whilst we relax in civilised comfort, the older children continue to run back and forth to the fairground, enjoying every minute of this new experience. It is just as well, because I do not feel it is bound to become a regular event on the calendar. But then – what does?

All this eating and drinking is bad for you, it is said. It is certainly worse for some than for others. Along with some eminent personalities in the farming hierarchy, he decides to go on a sponsored diet in order to help the needy in Africa. The yellow T-shirt, depicting the aforementioned gentlemen, is duly sent for and received.

'Not exactly your colour, dear, but I suppose that is hardly the object of the exercise.'

Yes, off he goes to his monthly NFU meeting looking like an ageing teddy bear, armed with sponsor forms and enthusiasm. The aim is to lose a stone in a month, a short sharp shock rather than a prolonged penance. His wife accompanies him for encouragement. A month seems a long time. We become experts on the qualities of grapefruit; no snap, crackle or pop for us in the mornings, the only noise being the rumblings of our insides. The intervals between meals seem much longer than before.

'Mummy, is it nearly tea-time?'

'No – another hour to go.'

'I wish we could put time on to fast forwards, don't you?'

I certainly do. It is for a good cause I continue to tell myself consolingly. Not only is it improving the quality of life of the African peasant but it should be having good effect on that of the Northumbrian one too. His outline is far from sylphlike and recent evidence suggests that, although an apple a day may be good for you, being shaped like one is not.

I become obsessed with food. It is not so bad for him as he is outside, away from it all most of the time – but we poor mortals cannot escape. We have to shop for it, put it into cupboards and fridge, cook it, clean it up off the table and floor . . . it is forever *there*. There develops a grim fascination about what goes down the alimentary tract of others:

'Did you not have your school dinner today?'

'Yes, but I am starving.'

At this, a couple of rolls, a banana and a yoghurt disappear by way of a light snack and then, unable quite to bridge the gap between tea and a supper of sausages, beans and mashed potatoes, he keeps hunger pangs at bay with a couple of bowls of Coco Pops!

'What did you have for lunch anyway?'

'Oh – er – corned beef salad, roast potatoes, a roll and, for pudding, apple pie and custard!'

The thought of all this actually has quite a nauseating effect but from time to time, the tempting vision of a chocolate biscuit hoves into view. . . .

The health food shop is not one of my regular ports of call, partly because of its inaccessibility by car – all-important with a young family. It is not the place to take young children anyway. Those bags of nuts, lentils, raisins and rice look too tempting for words, given the sheer joy of poking a chubby finger through the polythene and watching unmoved the resultant stream on to the floor. Therefore, when I do manage to escape into its murky interior, I tend to spend more time and money than necessary.

The labels on all shelves are written by hand in beautifully curly copperplate, the word 'organic' occurring frequently. It's all good stuff. In the same way that I think my muesli looks more wholesome on the table in an earthenware jar, those who care about food feel that commodities *not* purchased in nice, neat packaging, with attractive logos and nutritional information, must be better for you. Add to that the fact that everything is weighed in kilos instead of pounds, and you have the perfect recipe for parting people from their pence.

The place still has the power to fascinate and excite curiosity. Not only are there fruit and vegetables, and jars and bags of healthy food, herbs and spices, but there are also a rich array of homoeopathic balms and treatments, as well as shelf after shelf of beauty products guaranteed not to have been tested on animals. The latter bothers me slightly and I wonder if they have been tested at all; if not, the best you can expect is that the product has no effect.

Lost in a book on aromatherapy (living on a farm I can understand the power of a pong), I suddenly become aware of an elegant fellow customer in the shop, accumulating enormous quantities of Greek yoghurt, sunflower seeds, ginseng and oatmeal, and insisting upon the undivided attention of the rather flustered assistant.

'What do you recommend for indigestion?' she asks, eyeing the little bottles bearing Latin names. As she bundles up her purchases and prepares to leave, her leather handbag falls open and out falls quite the largest bar of chocolate I have ever seen. She does not meet my eyes as I hand it to her.

The water is brown. At least it is supposed to be water, and it is certainly coming from the tap on activation of the handle. Hot or cold, it looks the same, dyeing the washing brown and doing goodness knows what to our insides.

'It won't hurt you,' he says but we decide, on balance, we would prefer to drink brown liquid out of a bottle.

This state of affairs has arisen as a result of a broken water pipe. Someone ploughed too deep on a neighbouring farm. It is bad enough being without water for hours on end whilst waiting for that rare bird, an eager and athletic plumber, to heal the rift.

It would seem only decent to go along to the holiday cottage and explain the situation to this week's occupants. It has already been divined that he is an artist, and part of the reason they are staying in this part of the United Kingdom is that he has been exhibiting in Edinburgh. Sounds pretty impressive stuff. I duly trek up to the door of the cottage, a bottle of mineral under one arm and some Portuguese wine of dubious vintage under the other. 'Oh, you shouldn't have bothered,' she exclaims, accepting the offerings without emotion. 'How kind.'

When I come to do the cottage at the end of the week and remove the rubbish (the dustman cannot be persuaded to make a personal call) I discover that not only do their black bags clank but also there is a huge, empty cardboard case emblazoned with words in French, about appellation controlée, etc. I don't know why I bothered about the water (I certainly need not have worried about the wine); they probably never noticed its absence.

'What is a windfall, Mum?'

'It is when you receive a cash gift unexpectedly, like a legacy or winning the Pools, or something.'

'Oh – I see.'

This is a subject very dear to the heart of our eldest son. I would not say that he was mercenary, but when funds are low he has even offered to change the baby's nappy!

His eyes gleam in appreciation of his subject. He hates doing essays and we usually have to chain him to his desk, in conjunction with a serious threat – often associated with cash – until he has completed some sort of offering, his handwriting becoming increasingly large in order to meet the magic requirement of two pages. Not so today. He spends the entire evening happily scribbling, foregoing favourite TV programmes and well exceeding two pages.

This epic is a work of art that simply has to be read. Based loosely on the framework of 'his day', the action leaps forward at breathtaking pace – from the bus trip to school, straight into a maths class and reaching a spine-rattling climax at the dinner gong; at every turn, he more or less trips over a cache of fivers. Now on the way home from school, what should he perceive lying in the grass on alighting from the bus? Yes – you've guessed it. A gold nugget! He carries it into the house with difficulty as it is so heavy and – would you believe it? – it happens to have been mislaid by one or our bed-and-breakfast guests, who gives him a hundred pounds by way of a reward, in deep gratitude. His teacher writes her comment at the end of the essay: 'How many bed-and-breakfast guests do you have staying who carry gold nuggets?' Fair comment, if a bit hair-splitting.

As previously stated, the casualty department at the Infirmary is a well-known venue to this family. In a way, this is a good thing for if ever anyone wakes there from something serious, they will feel quite at home. The children know the system, they know where the toys are kept, they know where the comics are kept, they know the nurses (they have their preferences of course) and, naturally, they know our overworked GP.

Why are we here today? The answer is that, whilst father was in charge, he received a message from the sitting room where everyone was assembled ostensibly watching TV. A child had somehow become dislodged from the chair upon which he was sitting, quiet as a mouse, good as gold, was somehow propelled into the air, returning to earth via a small table, fashioned from a wooden beer barrel, catching his ear on the metal band as he passed. There are no totally reliable witnesses to the incident, least of all the victim. No matter, the result of this little acrobatic feat is the laceration of his left ear – quite a bad one.

'Hello, again. Who is it today?' comes the patient, resignedly cheerful voice of nurse. We like this one. 'Has he been here before?'

'Er . . . it is such a job to remember who has and who has not. Oh, yes – the last time was when he cut his lip falling off the kitchen table – and before that, he had a difference of opinion with barbed wire and before. . . .'

'OK, OK – it is just to check whether he has records here.'

We all have records here. Once, when left alone for a few moments, I read my own Casualty Card. It was a mistake.

'Dropped frozen salmon on toe!'

'Fly in ear.'

'Thinks she is in labour!'

'Don't worry. Doctor will soon be here.'

'We aren't worried.'

Far from it. The patient is engrossed in the *Beano Annual* (circa 1979). It is nice and warm, and I am absolved from the all-important decision of what to cook for supper. His father did offer to bring him but I volunteered on the excuse that I know the ropes. I know the ropes all right. Oh – good – they've changed the magazines since our last visit. I am just beginning to doze off when:

'Ah – there you are! At it again I see.'

'Oh, hello. Yes, an ear this time.'

'Oh good! I haven't done an ear for ages. Sorry you've stopped doing the eggs. What is the golf ball situation these days?' (When all other sources of income dry up, the older boys rise early at weekends in order to comb the nearby greens and environs for lost balls, which they subsequently exchange for profit.)

'I am sure I could rake up a few. I'll bring some in with me next time I come in.' (Imagining a child, distressed and bleeding being told to stand still whilst I looked for golf balls.)

The ear is now anaesthetised and the needle is being deftly threaded. A bit of a whizz kid with the needle is Scott. The patient lies on the bed, wide-eyed and trusting. See what I mean? It is a good thing to make frequent visits.

Finally, 'There we are: ten stitches. Is this a family record?'

'I do believe it is.'

The nurse smiles and adds with a touch of irony, 'I wonder how long it will stand?'

I have not fallen off a horse for ages. Not for at least eighteen months and that is with twice-weekly riding. I suppose I must have been becoming over-confident. Here we are – a sunny Sunday afternoon – one son and his middle-aged mama, plus four others, who seem fairly new to the sport, youngish and game. Charles and a groom officiate, one at the front and one at the back. All seems to be going smoothly. The horses seem to be lively but we are instructed to keep the pace sedate.

'Now, we are going down this bank to the bridge over the river. Take it slowly,' is the order.

I take it slowly but unfortunately the horse feels differently about this little challenge. The next thing I know is that I am on the bridge at one end and he has already traversed the river and is looking back at me without humour.

How humiliating! My loyal offspring is later to recount, with glee, that he turned round when he heard the scream (surely I didn't scream?) and was rather surprised, and I suspect rather embarrassed, to see his mother trying to reattach herself to the reins of the runaway horse.

I run painfully after the brute, who is now standing with the others as if butter wouldn't melt in his mouth. It is totally amazing what you do under stress. I am so angry with myself that I remount in one, instead of the usual groaning, arthritic reach.

'I thought you were going in for a swim,' grins one of our young companions. On our return home, my neck and shoulders are starting to stiffen.

'Bad way to fall off a horse,' declares my not-very-sympathetic spouse with shake of the head.

'Would you mind telling me which is the best way to fall off then?' I enquire acidly. As it is at least twenty years since he has been astride I do not feel he is in a position to give advice in this way.

Days later: 'You know, that bump on the head must have done you good. Look at all the work you have done this week!'

Spoken like a man! However, it is true that I have sorted out the attic after the mass exodus, 'done' the winter clothing, sorted out the dairy, the books, the toy cupboard. . . .

'Hello. Half-term? Family of four? Er, yes. . . .'

'What was that?' enquires my husband.

'Family of four for half-term.'

'Oh Christ. I took a booking for a family of three whilst you were out shopping this morning.'

We look at each other across the Formica-topped kitchen table.

'You know what *that* means?' I try not to allow my voice to tremble, take a frenzied dive for the bottle or throw china across the room.

'Yes, we'll all have to move back again.'

'It's only next week.' I cannot help a tear.

'Don't worry. You'll do it easily. It's not much.'

Not much? Only a small matter of moving the boys back up to the attics with all the items essential to their wellbeing, Lego, transformers, marbles, conkers, etc., then moving us back into their rooms with cot and clothes, bringing all the Bee-and-Bee bedding down from the attic cupboards. . . . This is all quite apart from polishing up the dining room and sitting room, removing all the Bee-and-Bee 'china' from our circulation (it has been such a luxury to have enough of everything). Not to mention the preparation of attractive, wholesome meals again rather than the ease of alternating omelettes with baked beans.

By the end of the week, I do have the house back to summer status once more. It has been a supreme effort.

I am totally exhausted but brainwashing myself to think of the money – an unscheduled addition to the coffers can be nothing but useful at this time of year. After all, we'll soon be in November, and after that, comes December. . . .

Mr and Mrs Smith arrive first on Saturday. They have the standard family of two, one of each, aged seven and nine. The children immediately mingle with ours as neither lacks confidence and although one is a girl (generally speaking, a dirty word) she soon proves pretty adept with a football, not to mention conkers or marbles – in fact, they soon forget she *is* a girl (supreme compliment). Once she has tired of the rougher end of the activity range, she sorts out the cassette box and shows pictures to the babes. This sort of behaviour is guaranteed to elevate any family staying here to a very high status. I feel bound thereafter to pull out all the stops and attend to their every whim.

'Scrambled eggs for the children in the morning? Not too runny? Certainly.' The beaming smile continues all the way back to the kitchen, instead of such a brief being received in stony silence with an eruption of rather rude language after the closing of the door which divides them from us, along the lines of, 'Where do these people think they are?' or 'Perhaps he'd like to come along and cook the blessed stuff himself?'

Later, even more unusual and praiseworthy, Mr Smith is to be found in the garden playing football with the boys. This family is rather special. Mrs Smith is sitting by the fire, reading. 'I feel so relaxed here,' she says. Oh, all that hard work was worthwhile.

Or was it? Lot Number Two do not arrive until late, which is a bit of a nuisance, to put it politely, as they require an evening meal. We greet them with beaming smile and show them to their rooms. The child is a girl of about eleven, with a pout, who looks utterly bored with the place already. However, they carry huge cases up to their rooms (how long did they say they were staying? It was only three nights, wasn't it?) presumably laden with books, cassettes, curling tongs, bottles of beauty lotions and cans of Coke.

I'll bet they are selective about what they eat too. Mother has a perpetually anxious expression on her face; she probably has 'bad nerves' and she'll worry about Emma's diet and how she is allergic to certain common substances. Father looks as if he wishes he'd booked in somewhere nearer the pub, if not actually inside it. Would I mind if they had a cup of tea first as they have had such an arduous journey from Yorkshire and need to unwind and steady their nerves?

I need to steady mine too but I feel that they would be quite impervious to the calming powers of tea. I return to the kitchen, take a large slug of sherry and mutter a few oaths reserved for contingencies like these. I open the oven door to inspect the pommes boulangères, or 'sliced potatoes' as they are rather commonly dismissed in this house. I do like the top to be browned but if the customers 'relax' much longer, the dish will be in serious danger of being unchewable and black.

I decide to take the pudding, cheese and salad in, and clatter around, breathing heavily, so that they realise that they are dealing with a force to be reckoned with. Of course, I have to wash their tea cups so that they can have a post-prandial cup of coffee. I cook the fish, down another glass of sherry and recklessly fling over a fistful of parsley. I love parsley, also it conceals a multitude of sins, in this instance, one or two of the fillets have actually disintegrated twixt pan and dish and, short of reaching for the glue, a nice green sprinkling covers the join.

I take in the dish, together with the well-cooked potatoes, similarly decorated (green and dark brown do look nice together). I call them bravely to the trough. . . .

They seem to spend hours over their meal. Just as I am thinking I'll just go to bed and *leave* everything, to hell with it all (but what about the washing up? There will be no dishes for breakfast), the door clicks. I enter yawning – ah well, it would be too much to expect to have two good 'lots' together. Perhaps they will decide the place is not suitable for them and go home tomorrow. . . .

I shall be glad when this diet is over. My reduced sugar level makes me very irritable; that's my story anyway. I wouldn't care but I have hardly lost any weight anyway. He has though, so it is all worthwhile – except that he is weak and irritable too. There is that nip in the air that heralds the winter and sharpens the appetite.

Gloom: Kevin signs off for the winter; the clocks turn back an hour; I have to move everyone back to winter quarters again. I repeat over and over to myself how I love the Aga, the comfortable bed, the electric blanket, the curtains, the carpet, the excuse not to do the garden. . . . Does this compensate for the long winter of short days in this draughty old house (new central heating system or not), during which time we hardly see a soul and everyone seems to catch one virus after another?

November

'We sometimes bring the children down to the beach near you,' remarks a chance acquaintance one day. 'They call it the End of the World.' As winter draws near, this description becomes increasingly apt.

However, what better place to hold a bonfire party? So think some of our friends, and the venue is instantly seized upon by all – including our children. For days beforehand, they toil tirelessly, collecting up odd bits of wood lying around. Had they been asked to collect kindling for the fire, the response would have been less than lukewarm. In no time at all, quite a pile is formed in the middle of the garden field.

In a fit of enthusiasm, I decide to clear out the potting shed, from which I can keep an eye on the young wood gatherers. Tray upon tray of cracked plastic seed pots are unearthed, as well as yards of rotting baler twine. There are bottles with illegible labels which had better be disposed of carefully, packets of seeds that should have been sown years ago, rusting garden tools of all shapes and sizes. Soon I can actually see the bench and floor of the shed. I stagger over to the fire, dusty and laden with rubbish. Come to think of it, there is an old chair in the house that can go on; better not search too strenuously or we shall end up with a denuded house.

'What about a guy?'

A pair of Daddy's old jeans and shirt are stuffed realistically but I have to say 'no' to the request to add a touch of realism to the face with his spare set of glasses. They complete the picture with woolly hat and gloves, then the lifesize figure, dressed more warmly than any of us glowing after our exertions, is hoisted, chair and all, on top of the mountain of wood and rubbish and tied into place with old baler twine. So far so good.

Now to turn our attention to the feeding arrangements. Even the most elaborate of bonfires and firework displays never lasts very long – never long enough for the cook to have ready the food for the chilled and hungry outdoor enthusiasts. Therefore I now find myself doing something which evokes the scorn of emancipated feminist friends – *preparation beforehand*. This is never an unqualified success either as the work has to be dovetailed with all the other demands on my time throughout the day.

'What are these?'

'Sausage rolls of course.'

'Ugh. They taste horrible.'

'I'm not surprised. I haven't cooked them yet.'

'Oooh, crisps!'

It never fails to impress or irritate that you can work your fingers to the bone and your imagination to its limits by producing platefuls of attractive cakes and biscuits for childrens' parties, and by and large, they will be left uneaten in preference for these highly flavoured salty offerings.

Leave them out, you might cry. But as far as 'they' are concerned, a 'do' is not a 'do' without crisps; every last crumb is always consumed.

'Leave them alone. The food is for *after* the fireworks.'

The offerings on the table are backed up by a big pan of rib-sticking soup, just the job for a chilly night. The trouble is that it is not chilly; we are in the throes of an exceptionally mild spell due to the greenhouse effect, I suppose. Moths are still flapping at the window and there are flies round the food, those plastic deterrents suspended from the ceiling last May having long lost their strength. For our liquid intake there are several crates of beer and Coke, and also a commendable concoction on the cooker, again against the chill night air, called 'Gluhwein'. It smells yuk; I think I must have overdone the cloves.

Ah – here comes someone. Car lights illuminate the yard. And another . . . and another. Suddenly, the kitchen is full of voices. Out of the corner of my eye, I can see the crisps disappearing. The beer is going down too, a little anaesthesia must be felt necessary before facing the fireworks. We have a motley crew here – several teachers, a wine merchant, a rock band manager, a doctor . . . er, what was that? Farmers? No – no farmers.

They dutifully all move outside. It is not that I don't want to see the fireworks or the guy, or that I feel bound to stay and stir the soup, but the very young actually don't like the bangs and flashes in the dark. The sulphurous smell is enough for me. Two or three breaths of that and I am transported straight back to childhood, when fireworks seemed so much bigger and better and lasted longer. Outside, everyone is very impressed with the guy, it seems almost a shame to burn him. Inside, I remove the sausage rolls from the oven and get mugs for the soup.

Here they come. At a rough head count, there seem to be thirty-four children and twelve adults.

By 10 pm everyone has gone home. The kitchen looks as if it has been driven through by a JCB, the smell of smoke hangs on the air, inside and out.

'Great place for a bonfire,' everyone says. I don't mind the bonfire but I think the 'aprés ' can take place somewhere else another year.

Back in the garden, having completed the 'nice' job of sorting out the flower beds and planting wallflowers for the spring, attention has to be turned to the more vigorous exercise. The tedious task that crops up every spring and autumn is the strawberry patch although, if the yield is anything like it was this year, it hardly seems worth the effort. Here we go, wheelbarrow at the ready. I know it is not really wise to crawl on hands and knees across the soil. Baggy brown patches appear on the good trousers I forgot to change, but I maintain that crawling and weeding on hands and knees is far better for the back (not to mention the soul) than bending.

Next, there is the vexed question of the digging. It is better at this time of year if you can arrange for this to be followed by a frost to complete the operation. A few years ago, when I began to read gardening books I was astonished to learn that a process known as double-digging should be undertaken here. This was a complete revelation and quite honestly, knowledge I felt better to be without. Rather like herring-boning a hem; you know it makes a better job but you have neither the time nor the patience, so you stick to the slip-stitch (slipshod stitch in my case) which has stood you in good stead for years. Yes, I am afraid my digging consists of turning over the soil.

Sometimes – and I do feel guilty about this – Kevin does it. I do not know what method he employs but he makes a far better job than I do.

Well, he has made it. Off he goes to the NFU meeting minus a stone and ready to collect the cash. He is pleased with himself, looks less like a teddy bear and looking forward to the first pint he has had for a month.

When one diet ends, another begins:

'It's one thing being on Death Row but this is – well – purgatory. We are all brought in last week and "him from the mart" joins the act, poking and prodding us around. As usual, one group goes off in the wagon but us – those that you can see here – all ten of us – are ushered into this little – well, I wouldn't call it a field, would you? "Too fat" they said, "you'll have to go on a diet." '

'Which method did they follow? Cambridge Diet? The F-Plan?'

'F-Plan? No – we have just been left here with nowt but water for the week. I shouldn't be surprised if we are too thin now.'

'Well, there you are! If you are too thin, you'll have to stay on another week, and at least you'll have plenty to eat.'

'I say, are you thinking what I am thinking? We could swing this for weeks. Anything is better than ending up on the plate.'

'The NFU Dinner? I thought you didn't like all-male do's?'

'I've told everyone you will not let me go – so I'll have to go in order to protect your reputation.'

And they talk about feminine logic! I must record in my defence that his track record for this particular event is poor – to put it mildly. On the last occasion, the phrase 'roaring drunk' comes to mind but really this could hardly describe the figure of shambling pathos which poured itself into the kitchen around midnight.

The time before, I was ill – yes, the farmer's wife and mother of many, dared to be ill. Undaunted, he set off, whistling, leaving the usual early evening chaos with an 'I'll not be late' thrown over his shoulder. He was still whistling when he returned at 3.30 am, by which time the entire county police force had been alerted, not to mention all casualty departments in the area – and his wife was almost in need of hospitalisation herself.

Never mind – he's off again. Here he comes, jumping down the stairs, newly shaved, looking better dressed than he has done for months.

He returns at approximately 12.26 am.

'I'm quite sober. I stuck to beer tonight.'

I would have found this intelligence more comforting if the night (what was left after he had told me who was there and who had said what to whom) had not been punctuated by frequent visits to the loo, leaving wife exposed and cold. He has the unique facility of being able to fall instantly and deeply asleep between trips. His wife does not. It doesn't seem fair that breakfast sees him crunching his cornflakes chirpily whilst I feel like death.

Gordon, the garage proprietor, works hard and plays hard, one of a dying breed, in contrast with the occupants of the holiday cottage this week who jog and swim every day, avoiding stimulants stronger than raspberry leaf tea. Another pair arrived from far-off Sussex, with two canoes strapped to the car roof, not to mention two fold-up bikes inside. Is this enjoying yourself I ask? Ah well – chacun à son goût.

Gordon does enjoy himself. It is not much out of his way to pay us a visit as we are so close to his 'home from home', the golf course. Not only does he enjoy swinging his arm but also lifting it – and why not? Raspberry leaf tea indeed!

However, when working, he puts heart and soul into the job in hand. On one famous occasion whilst I was speeding to the airport with my mother to collect dear brother and his family, the car appeared suddenly to give up the ghost. It was a Saturday morning. One simple telephone call and out came Gordon on his dashing white charger, well Hillman Avenger actually.

'You take this and I'll take that,' he ordered.

We continued on our way in warmth, comfort and style and Gordon limped home in the battered old Volvo (B.O.V.) which he had sorted out and ready for our return.

He is a good sort is Gordon and the reason he is sitting at our kitchen table today is to discuss the possible purchase of a new car. No, we are not going to relinquish our beloved B.O.V. but it does seem to use a good deal of petrol and, since the number of occupants frequently falls to four, a smaller car would do local trips with ease. Now it just so happens that Gordon has the very thing in his showroom at the moment; it is perhaps a little younger than what we had in mind and thus a little more expensive, but well, in the long run. . . .

To cut a long story short, we take it and I now drive through the town quite anonymous. Everyone knew the B.O.V., this little 'metallic' green Metro is not what people expect to see transporting Fraters from A to B. It is quite astonishing how many children it holds. I would not say that all of them are sitting in comfort but, they are in. All the instruments work and we are making a determined effort not to despoil the upholstery. The foam headrests of the Volvo were just too tempting.

'Why did you do it?'

'I couldn't help it.'

Yes, this is a neat little number, Gordon has done us proud. We justify it by declaring that we do actually need two cars. When a child is bleeding profusely, having fallen off the henhouse roof, it is irksome, not to mention distressing or messy, to have to wait for a parent to return from a trip before medical attention can be sought.

Mother is on holiday again, in Majorca. The dog seems to be steering clear of trouble this time. Yes, my mother is a much-travelled lady who has been halfway round the world by herself dozens of times – well, at least four. For shorter hauls like the current one, she has the entire process down to a fine art. She and her friend, Alice, steam the sixty miles or so down the A1 in her bright green Mini to the airport, from where Alice's son collects the car and looks after it in their absence. On their return, the Mini does a reverse performance. This all seems very satisfactory and involves no one at this end. So, having received our usual entitlement of illegible post cards and letters, we now await the phone call to announce her safe return to her village a few miles away.

'I've had a bit of an accident.' She imparts the information tremulously, her voice far removed from its usual resonance.

'What happened?'

'Well, Alice and I went out with this couple who had hired a car, and well . . . we had a crash.'

'Are you all right?'

'Yes. I spent the whole of the second week in hospital, though.'

'Why didn't you let us know?'

'I didn't want to bother you.'

This obviously demands closer scrutiny than the telephone will give at this state of the art.

Someone resembling Cheko The Giant Panda greets me at

191

the door. Yes, they were really quite nice at the hospital. She did have quite severe concussion though.

A thought suddenly occurs to me.

'How did you get home from the airport?'

'I drove.'

'For goodness sake. . . .'

Words fail me for several moments. 'You really shouldn't have,' I manage at last. 'Can you see properly?' Her eyes, swollen and surrounded by bruised and blackened flesh do not look too promising.

'Not too bad, but I do tend to get double vision.'

There are some fortunate folk driving on the roads, it is just as well they are unaware of their lucky escape.

'Why didn't you phone us?' I groan.

'Oh, it would have been too complicated and besides – you are too busy.'

Too busy! I am gradually receiving the message that my presence is superfluous. She has another visitor bearing gifts, edible ones, whilst I feel conscious of my empty hands. The children are annoying her. When my mother is well, she tolerates the children; when she is ill, she hardly notices them; when she is semi-ill, like now, they irritate her in the extreme. Unfortunately, it is to be many weeks before she is truly well again.

'You'll end up just like her,' declares an independent observer, whom I had hitherto regarded as a friend. 'Women always do.'

We are gradually getting used to Kevin being off for the winter. It affects our lives quite a lot. On the credit side, it means that the boss does not have to be breakfasted and out by 8 am, not that he always was anyway, but he did try. Also, lunch does not have to be on the table at twelve, which it certainly never was – and hasn't been since the first week of married life.

On the other hand, it does mean we have sole responsibility, not only are we the boss but also the worker. We have to do the routine jobs like feeding and bedding inside, fencing when a weakness appears in defences, and all the other rotten, boring jobs on top of the daily trek round the fields. It means that there is less time spent in the house and he does not keep quite so well abreast of current affairs: there are days when he has to give the personal column a miss. Never mind, this additional exercise will be just what is required to maintain the new sylphlike shape.

From time to time, roles are swapped. Well, not quite. When he looks after the children, that is more or less what he does, in conjunction with reading the papers, of course. There is naturally no question of there being time to stack the dirty dishes in the machine, or peel the potatoes for lunch or hang out the washing. It must be quite a cushy little job he has. . . .

When the reserve shepherd returns, however, after being subjected to a careful interrogation concerning the status quo sheepwise, she has to cast aside her shepherd's cloak, don her apron and put her mind and body to the preparation of suitable midday refreshment. Not to mention, clearing all remaining traces of the last, putting in a load of washing, pegging one out and generally attempting to restore order.

As far as the sheep are concerned, the reserve shepherd actually earns some praise today, by extracting four ewes from a field of wheat single-handed, without dog. I am rather proud of this technique, perfected over years of intermittent sheep management. What you do is this. You enter the field in question very quietly and then slowly begin to approach the offenders laterally. You start talking to them quietly once you are within earshot; up go their heads as they listen, unblinking. It may still take a while to move them out of the field but patience is all.

'Here she comes. She is going off her head, poor soul. That's what comes after years of living with him of course. What can you expect? What on earth is she on about? We know we shouldn't be in this field. We aren't daft but, believe me, if you had the choice of quietly nibbling in a nice

> new field of wheat or being chased round by those lecherous
> brutes in there, what would you do? It's commonsense,
> isn't it? People think we sheep are stupid, that we haven't
> minds of our own. . . . Oh well, she seems on the verge
> of tears, begging us to come quietly and move towards
> the gate. She is teetering on the brink all right. I think
> we had better humour her for once, instead of the usual
> dance we lead her for hours. I still laugh to think of the
> time when she spent ages getting some of us out of the
> field and then – put us in with the Blackies! I bet she had
> a telling-off that day. Right-o, then, girls, here we go – the
> gate!'

Despite all adversity, I manage a couple of evenings out. One
is to a local women's group I occasionally attend. The subject
tonight is Colour Coding. Colour coding? The hypothesis on
which this therapy is based is that everyone should wear a
certain set of colours, according to their colouring (which
again is coded to the seasons, but this is really irrelevant). I
don't know about anyone else but I should have thought that
this is fairly obvious. Apparently not.

It's a nice little money-spinner, imported from over the
Atlantic. The operator/consultant visits people or hosts them
for a session and the proceedings are conducted with great
aplomb, against a plain background screen. It is all designed
to improve the appearance and subsequent well-being of the
client, and I daresay that many a farmer's wife wilting under
the strain would benefit from such a consultation. The object
of this particular evening is to demonstrate the artistry of
the operator to us poor ordinary mortals, most of us clad in
quite the wrong hue – whatever came to hand in our rush
to escape.

Secondly, at the big school there is a production of 'Joseph
and his Amazing Technicolour Dreamcoat.' When it comes
to educational offerings, I usually draw the short straw of
doubtful privilege. I have to take all the children, apart from
baby and one invalid. We crane our necks on uncomfortable

seats after the obligatory waving across the hall to various acquaintances.

'Can we move to . . .?'

'Look, there's Richard over there. Can I . . .?'

'No. No. No. We are staying here. Shut up.'

The play is performed with cheerful enthusiasm and confidence with no costume or props apart from the coat. It is rather good and the children watching, especially the younger ones, tap their hands and feet to the compulsive rhythms. Nonetheless, I am glad when it is over and always remember words overheard many years ago whilst filing out after a definitely more ambitious (and lengthier) offering:

'What did you think of it?'

'Lovely dear. Tedious, but . . . lovely.'

There is a great deal of interest in colour in the field. Even in these technological times, the principles employed to ensure the appearance of large numbers of lambs in the spring are very simple and unchanged since life began – and the monitoring thereof even simpler. In those far-off urban days of ignorance I can't recall questioning the appearance of technicolour bottoms on sheep at this time, neither did I see that the 'daddy sheep' wore a harness; I must have been protected from such hard facts of life. Some lucky ladies manage to exhibit all three colours at the end of three weeks.

> *'Good grief! What colour does he call that?'*
>
> *'What?'*
>
> *'I mean, have you seen the colour of your back end?'*
>
> *'Of course I haven't. I am not double-jointed or perverted.'*
>
> *'The boss has just been down to change the harness. What was wrong with the old blue, red and green; that's what I want to know?'*
>
> *'Well, what colour is it for goodness sake?'*
>
> *'I suppose you'd call it vermillion.'*
>
> *'Vermillion? What sort of colour is that? Oh-oh, look out; here he comes – Randy Robert, King of the Rams.'*

*   *   *

'Could we book in for a couple of nights, bed and breakfast, please?'

'Double room?'

'Er, lovely, yes.' Bed and breakfast in November. They must be mad.

'And evening meal?'

I suppose so. Christmas is looming up ahead and any extra income is always welcome.

'I've been before.'

'Oh yes?'

'I've been a few times actually. Golf. John Murphy is the name. I am getting married.'

Getting married! Why don't they go abroad?

'We haven't much time. We've only got the weekend.'

Weekend! Honeymoon in tatty old farmhouse in Northumberland in November! I ask you? Where has all the romance gone in life?

Here they are, smiling and covered in confetti. At least some traditions continue. They are duly fed and settle down in front of the roaring fire so necessary at this bleak time of year.

'Er, excuse me. You don't happen to have a pack of cards, do you?'

We trudge on through what I consider the most miserable month of the year. I know the winter months are often colder but November becomes increasingly dark, the days shorten and are often full of mist and fog. How often do I stagger back to the car with the shopping, only to find that the lights have been left on and the wretched thing is sitting there, drained of life? A new washing machine is purchased at last because the old one is drained of life too; if the washing machine does not work, the whole fabric of our life grinds to a halt.

In all this damp, depressing greyness, a sudden cold snap is quite welcome. The chilly winds whip up a creamy confection in the sky, and suddenly it starts to snow. In no time, the ground is covered and the children race outside in excitement, ready to play.

It is Sunday and I decide not to cancel my regular ride, my mother regarding me strangely over her glasses again. True to form, the depth and intensity of the snow increases as I head inland. On I plod, you could hardly call it driving. Perhaps my mother was right. Blinding clouds of snow rush towards me and there seems to be a thick carpet on the road. Road? What road? Perhaps I had better turn back, I do have my maternal responsibilities to consider after all.

Yes, I turn back and retrace my wheelmarks. There does not seem to be much traffic about. A bit eerie really. Hello – what's that? Up above the billowing white clouds there is blue sky; it must be clearing. To hell with it. I do a rather spectacular three-point skid and proceed to the stables.

The horse chosen to bear me today seems quite surprised at this turn up for the books. Let's face it, even this far north we do not get a lot of snow really. The group of riders who comprise the party I am to join suddenly appear out of the swirling flakes. They have already been out for an hour, as I can tell from their scarlet complexions and rather fixed grins. Charles is wearing a scarf tied round his hard hat, which detracts a little from his elegant bearing.

Never mind, here we go, into a field for my first canter across the snowy waste. No, it's a gallop – clarts of mud flying everywhere. This is the stuff. It gets the old circulation going. Suddenly, the snow stops altogether and the sky clears completely; it is still cold but wonderfully invigorating. Who needs massage, aromatherapy, colour coding? We have a really splendid hour – lots of what Charles calls 'little canters'.

Now, what is happening? Charles is addressing the only male member of the group, devising some sort of complicated arrangement. Why is it that men automatically think that only other men can understand things? Quite frankly, in this case, I rather doubt if anyone can understand what Charles has up his sleeve for us. We remain in the dark. Male rider

197

mutters something to us about turning the horses out for the night in this field behind some woodland. Charles and the youngest member of the party go trotting home. No, I still haven't grasped it.

One by one, we untack our mounts and turn them into a field which looks like less than five-star accommodation, but the horses don't seem to mind – probably only too glad to get the heavy bodies off their backs. Here we are then: a party of five standing in the middle of nowhere, at the edge of a field of wheat, weighed down with saddle and bridle. I am still bemused.

Ah – all is revealed! Here comes Charles in his car, which makes our B.O.V. look like a Rolls. It appears to be held together with mud or worse and is filled with bales of hay. He drives at great speed down the slippery and rutted track and screeches to a halt near the gateway to the horses' field. If we were not spattered with mud before, we certainly are now.

Charles leaps out of the car and loads himself up with bales. Without another utterance he proceeds into the fields where he distributes the hay for the hungry horses. This little ritual lasts quite ten minutes, during which time the horseless riders stand holding their tack, feeling helpless and rather foolish. At last:

'Right-O. Well done.' He strides briskly back to the car, flinging a loud 'Come on!' over his shoulder. The car is the type which has a rear door and we are instructed to place our saddles there. As one bends one's head to do so, one is hit physically by a powerful smell – could it be a mixture of leather, petrol, manure, straw, and probably one or two other ingredients difficult to isolate and probably just as well? After the saddles, there is scant room in the rear.

'You two sit in there!' orders Charles to the gentleman and his lady.

'Er – how . . . where . . .?'

'Just hang your legs out. Shan't close the door.'

'Oh.'

Two ladies sit in the rear passenger seat in relative comfort, although as this is the nucleus of the vehicle, the pong is strongest. One lady sits in the front passenger seat. She has hardly had time to swing in her legs before the clutch is released with a jerk and we are off.

I have travelled in a number of different vehicles and modes of transport in my time but this is something else. We jolt up and down horrendously and not surprisingly are swathed in a cloud of petrol fumes. Those in the rear choke a bit and protest as well as they are able about possible poisoning.

'Oh – no fear of that,' chortles Charles with confidence, 'it's lead-free petrol!' He is grinning from ear to ear and it occurs to me that he does not actually like people much. The lady in the front seat tries to relax as she is thrown from side to side over an exposed spring. The door of the glove compartment flies open, exposing a cavity filled with straw. 'There used to be a mouse's nest in there,' says Charles cheerfully. This news has quite a dramatic effect on the lady in front. She is quite a large lady; otherwise, I think she would have climbed over into the back with us – smell or no smell. The remainder of the journey back to the farm takes place in silence, everyone deep in their own thoughts.

We are approaching the silly season: bazaars, Christmas fayres, bring-and-buy sales abound, in order to capitalise on the pre-Christmas fever. There are big, efficiently organised affairs held in the town hall or community centre, run by committees of ladies of excellence, often farmers' wives, united in their desire to raise funds for favourite charities. There are the school efforts. Then, there are the minority group gatherings, like this one to which I have been urged to attend this morning. Oddly enough, there is a fair sprinkling of farmers' wives in this organisation too, young radicals, free thinkers.

I wonder to which end of the spectrum I am nearest and I have plenty of time to speculate as, having been ushered into this room of pleasing dimensions, I am alone. The only furniture I can see is a grand piano and a racing bicycle.

'Where shall I put the things I have brought?' I enquire into thin air.

The pale-faced lady, with pale blue eyes behind her rimless glasses, reappears and gestures silently with a limp white wrist towards the piano. I place my pile of children's clothes beside the other two items: a carefully worked cloth elephant and a rather sad looking chocolate cake.

The vision disappears again. What do I do now? Is it my imagination or do I hear the clinking of cups and voices upstairs? Come to think of it, the invitation did read, 'bring-and-buy sale and coffee morning'.

I come to a decision. It's cold in this room, but only a few doors away lives the godmother of one of my children, a dear friend of long standing. I back out down the long passage clutching toddler and baby, and run as fast as I can under the circumstances.

'Oh, thank goodness you are in!'

'Lovely to see you! Come in! Have a drink!'

She is like that. It is only 11 am but I rather think I shall accept this hospitality; I could do with warming up. I'll be late home for lunch of course but what's new? And what is more – what is new in town?

'Not much. . . . I suppose you heard about . . .? Have I seen you since . . .? We settle down, glass in hand. Lunch certainly will be late today.

It is Saturday and the children are more than usually annoying. Serves you right for having so many, I hear you say. Well, in my experience, even the smallest family has its moments. It is a damp and gloomy day. There is a good deal of internal friction from the moment they drift downstairs, bleary-eyed, to watch 'Wacaday'. You hate yourself for allowing them to watch it and feel you should be more forceful, but quite honestly, you haven't the strength and besides – what would they be doing if they were not watching it?

Exactly! Generally speaking, all those aged four and over

watch spellbound and the resultant silence is the lull before the storm that is Saturday. Those under the age of four, which in this house number two, soon lose interest and have to be found alternative amusement.

Naturally, the fact that it is Saturday means nothing to the farmer and today seems even busier than a 'normal' day. Late last night, dear brother-in-law phoned (how I'd like to wring his neck) to announce the arrival of a wagon at 8 am for his cattle which we have been grazing for some weeks, because of his lack of grass. Therefore, 'Daddy' is out pretty promptly, even before 'Wacaday'. Therefore, there is a squad clad in pyjamas and unbreakfasted lying around mesmerised in the sitting room, whilst their mother remains in the kitchen feeding baby and humouring her three-year-old daughter who is 'not quite right'. It's probably a virus – a touch of the 'a-lot-of-it-abouts'.

There is a horrendously cheerful travel programme on the radio which I feel bound to switch off, but then what is left is undiluted moaning and crying. I think perhaps baby is cutting a tooth, the cornerstone of diagnosis in this house for the first few years of life. A little Mozart on cassette might help – soothing and hypotensive. That's better. One of the TV people returns to the kitchen coughing and wheezing.

'Have you taken your "machines" this morning?' He's a known asthmatic, and this word is more 'fun' than 'inhaler'.

The answer is a series of body-racking paroxysms, a case for the nebuliser to pump clouds of magic gas into the unfortunate sufferer by way of tube and mask – much to the alarm of onlookers, strangers visiting, Bee and Bees, etc. He accepts this with a resignation borne of the knowledge that it makes him better, for a while. On the other hand, there is no magic answer for teething babies, at least I have never found one.

Oh – oh, there goes the phone. It is Jack.

'Is there anything you want from the Cash and Carry?'

You know the feeling. Your mind goes totally blank and you know perfectly well that the minute you put the phone down, you will think of something.

'Oh that's kind of you, Jack. They don't do megasized bottles of Calpol I suppose?'

(To anyone without young children I would explain that Calpol is a horribly smelling sticky substance which contains a magic ingredient guaranteed to cure all ills. For a start – they love it. The consistency of this concoction bears no resemblance to anything else ever encountered. You think there is little left in the bottle; you tip it sharply over an angle of 90 degrees and – no, it does not rush out spilling all over the place. It fills the spoon, the surplus slowly running over on the floor before insertion into the willing wide-open mouth. How did we manage without it?)

However, Jack and I conclude that Calpol is only obtainable from the chemist. He suggests magnums of tomato ketchup, oven chips, beefburgers, potato waffles. . . . I am tempted. Heaven knows I am tempted, but somehow to buy vast quantities of such substances would seem the surrender of all the values I hold dear. The odd purchase now and again, when it seems either that or certification, is another thing.

In the end, I mumble off a few items like coffee and cornflakes and replace the phone. I wish I could go to the place myself, especially today. Meanwhile – bad news – 'Wacaday' appears to have finished. They all fall into the kitchen, blinking.

'Go and get dressed, you lazy lot,' I shriek.

'You aren't!'

Oh, they are quite right. It is definitely one of those days. We all dress quickly and then they start demanding breakfast. The cereals are in fact still standing on the table but, no, it is Saturday.

'Can we have: sausages/a boiled egg/bacon . . .?'

By the time this meal is completed, he is back from the fields and muttering about coffee. Whereas most of the jobs in this house are 'hers', making coffee is 'his' job generally speaking and this is not to be sniffed at.

Hardly has he swallowed the last mouthful when the 'bell'

goes. It is Kevin. There are some cattle out again – have to fix that fence.

Inside we limp through till lunchtime when the pinnacle of culinary achievement is presented on the table: sausages and mashed potatoes with or without beans (no choice). There is many a day when I cook one meal for them, one meal for him and one for himself. Not today. Afterwards, he goes off to repair the fence. It looks brighter outside now, with a flicker of wintry sunshine; just as well as it will soon have gone down altogether. Not that it matters much. Those who are well are fighting; those not so well are crying. Mozart is losing ground fast. At last I snap.

'Get yourselves outside!' I shriek hysterically – more hysterically than I thought. *Everyone* is now outside, except baby.

After a few minutes I feel a little guilty about this. It is chilly. Half of them are not well. They have no coats on. I rap sharply on the window to attract their attention. Obviously I am still full of pent-up emotions because – I go straight through the glass! For ten seconds, there is total silence at the sight of this huge hole in the kitchen window and then – great hilarity.

'Wait till Daddy . . .'

He comes back at last, having been briefed outside by a gleeful group.

'Why don't you go for a walk, dear? Have some fresh air? A breather?'

Soon I am striding across the beach, well, walking anyway, the cool air stinging my cheeks. You know, I am sorry to see the back of the swallows and house martins but there is something quite magical about the call of the curlew. Here we are – to right or left, not a living soul, or sign of life.

Small wonder those children call it the end of the world.

December

'Mummy, where do we come from?' The large, earnest eyes of our six-year-old philosopher meet mine. Oh no, not that again surely? I take a deep breath and begin my standard simplified version. He soon interrupts. 'No, what I mean is – don't we have to go back there to be counted?'

Yes, it's *that* time of year. It is a strange time if you are a farmer's wife with young children. On the farming side, with the days so short, work is largely whittled down to routine-only jobs. In contrast, on the non-farming side, everything is anything but routine. This is a frantically busy period for mothers. There seem so many jobs to complete before you-know-when: clandestine trips to town when you can never get exactly what you want; the writing of cards and letters (correspondence has been reduced to an annual activity), the exhausting process of present-wrapping. . . .

They do not seem to have actually done anything at school for weeks. Life seems to be a succession of plays, parties and trips I reflect, as I sit in the car one chilly evening awaiting the return of the bus from Newcastle which will discharge my child, amongst others, after a performance of 'The Wizard of Oz'. In reply to my question as to whether he enjoyed this particular production, I receive the standard answer:

'It was great on the bus.'

It is surely a paradox to someone who spent twenty-odd years of her life stepping from bus to bus that she should produce a family for whom such travel is a magical experience. The school mini bus of course does not count.

Now, having a ride in the cab of a lorry is even better than a bus. I can understand that. Uncle John has come over to take away his ewe hoggs, which have been enjoying an extended stay in our fields. As the operation has to be conducted in two parts, certain members of the family seize the opportunity with both hands. It is a bizarre sight when they return: a lorry cab full of elaborately party-hatted heads, blowing hooters and waving streamers. They are full of mischief and sweets; they have obviously been over-indulged by this fond, favourite relative.

'We like going to Uncle John's farm,' they say. They always omit the mention of his calves, sheep, dogs, etc., which they are bound to be shown. They are too busy detailing the excellence of the chocolate cake, the scones or the strawberry jam. All right, all right – I know baking and the making of preserves are not my strong point. If it were, it wouldn't be such a treat to eat the occasional 'proper tea' would it?

A child has been sick in the car. This leads you to a bit of a dilemma. Should you wind down the window and inhale the extremely powerful aroma of a neighbour's muck-spreading or should you grin and bear it? As we have only a short distance to travel now, we opt for the latter. This neighbour winters his cattle on slats, and the resultant slurry is particularly potent. It is dispersed energetically by means of a machine which rejoices in the title of 'side-flinger' – an apt name as it seems to the passing observer that the stuff could not be more widely distributed if it had been scooped up in handfuls and dealt with by the world's fastest spin bowler. You certainly feel a lot safer in the car than out.

Ah – the air smells sweet up here on top of the moors. I am escaping again for another hour of therapy . . . mind clearance . . . horse riding . . . call it what you will, lucky that my nearest and dearest can adjust his day to allow my absences.

This afternoon, the party consists of a rather proficient young lady, a rather nervous lady and a young gentleman somewhere between the two. We are in the care of Gemma, the groom, who appears to be slightly disgruntled from the start, for reasons undisclosed. She constantly reprimands P.Y.L. for springing into action before she has completed delivery of her orders. I have previously ridden the mount that P.Y.L. has and, much as you like to ride something which goes when you want him to go, he has the unfortunate tendency to go when you do not.

There is little the slight sympathetic rider can do about it. There is no malice in him really but when he hears Gemma say, 'Now what I want you to do is . . .', he pricks up his ears and finishes her sentence for her, adding a few equine epithets of his own.

What she was actually going to say was, '. . . trot to the corner of the field and then canter gently along the hedgerow up to the top. . . .'

George, however, was quite certain she was going to say, '. . . gallop madly up to the top of the field from here!'

P.Y.L., I learn later during the course of the ride, is reading Russian and other subjects at Oxford but luckily she seems also to have been blessed with an astonishingly thick skin. She enjoys her ride. The nervous young woman remains silent throughout. The young gentleman does not say a great deal. He is a Minister of the Church and although he answers pleasantly, I suspect he is spending most of the ride praying.

Once we reach the top of the hill, we can see right across the valley to the hills on the other side – and beyond. It is an awesome sight, especially in the strange light that these short days bring. Down the other side we go.

'Shut the gate, Veronica!'

Now this particular piece of acrobatics is not, I am ashamed to say, yet part of my repertoire. I lean precariously backwards trying to catch the gate as I come through; this is not a success. Gemma explodes. 'How not to shut a gate!' she announces loudly to the assembled company patiently waiting, whilst the culprit tries to blend into the background foliage.

We proceed in silence. I wonder what the horses are thinking. There is a school of thought, widely held by farmers, that horses are stupid creatures for allowing themselves to be tamed and submitting to the bit. But despite this harnessing of power for human purpose a personality still shines through. I am learning this, and certainly these little girls who like nothing better than to spend all their free time looking after them would fiercely champion the cause of 'horses are intelligent beings.'

I am riding the oldest horse in the stable today. He is a lovely old man, quiet and placid for the timid and yet game for the gallops if that is what you want. At all events, everyone has to admit that horses are surely more intelligent than sheep which, generally speaking, lack the individualist approach. I suppose we shall never know whether, having trained a nice strong Suffolk to the bit, he would jump a gate or gallop like a good 'un.

Back at the ranch we have a happy event, a little premature but exciting nonetheless. It is twins, apparently, and first report declares mother and babes to be doing well. However, examination two days after birth reveals the smaller of the two to be losing body heat and to be becoming rather lethargic.

The first I hear about this change in condition is when he comes into the kitchen.

'Have you got a box?'

'What sort of box? What size?'

My mind is on other things. I am suddenly aware that he is holding a small woolly creature under his arm and close inspection shows it to be a not very well woolly creature. Ah yes – that sort of box. After all it is some months since I have been faced with this problem. Some thought is required. Eventually, some Christmas decorations unearthed from the attic are emptied into two carrier bags, and a suitable box is accepted.

The lamb is now set to simmer in the oven. Within two hours it is dead. The children are quite upset about it. They haven't developed the thick skin of March and April when a four-year-old can be heard to pipe: 'Is it dead, yet, Daddy?'

As far as I am concerned, this earlier-than-usual start to the season cannot be anything but a nuisance.

Their garage bears a striking resemblance to a rather dimly lit 'fruiterers and poulterers'. My sister-in-law cannot contain herself at auctions, she has a severe addiction problem. This is understandable to a degree, for there is nothing like the excitement generated by bidders, whether it is a pedigree tup or a china vase going under the hammer. In this case, it has obviously been poultry and vegetables. In the run-up to Christmas, such affairs abound at local marts and she has, as usual, been carried away. Her mother has the enigmatic fixed smile on her face we know so well and she slowly shakes her head to complete her disapproval.

There seem to be, as far as I can make out, half a dozen chickens, four capons, two ducks, a goose . . . and a partridge in a . . .? No, no partridge, not as far as I can see anyway. Then, there are sacks of potatoes, turnips, sprouts, carrots . . . not to mention a huge basket of mushrooms.

'Would you like some vegetables?'

'Yes, please.'

My mother-in-law has disappeared. She returns with several capacious carrier bags into which she is soon ladling large quantities with gusto. 'I expect other members of the family will take some too,' I suggest at last. 'I hope so,' she replies with a grimace. The garage still looks as if they are set for a siege.

'What's that? You won't be going to the dinner on Thursday? Hugh has knocked his teeth out playing squash? Oh dear.'

'Someone' is not very sympathetic. 'I always said squash was a daft game. All these things; jogging, etc. . . .'

'It's all right for you, dear. You have an active outdoor job (some of the time anyway). People have to take exercise if their jobs are sedentary. It's a question of health.'

'Health be blowed. More like a good excuse to go to the pub afterwards if you ask me!'

'You are just jealous because you get adequate exercise at your work. . . .'

It seems that our friend was rushed to hospital where the errant choppers were replaced and the instructions imposed that no solid food is to go past them for at least a month. At this time of year! I bet he could spit! No perhaps not. This is all very serious and he feels understandably down. Not only will he miss our annual 'do' but neither will he be able to get his mouth round his Christmas dinner. He soon bounces back, driving his wife potty, creating nourishing soups and purées with which to sustain himself.

'One of us' grumbles a bit about going to the annual dinner of the local women's group. 'There are no farmers to talk to. You can't have a decent conversation with anyone. . . .'

Over the years I have been to about four 'farming do's' – parties, dances, it doesn't make any difference – at approximate intervals of about five years, the philosophy being that in our absence, things will have improved. They will not have done. What happens is that, within a short time, the company settles to form two strata, the division being that of sex. What I have found is that if I remain talking to my own sex, I run out of conversation in about two minutes and spend the rest of the evening trying to invent ways to escape. If I adopt a more aggressive stance, determined not to conform, I drink too much and cannot remember what I or anyone else has said afterwards. Either way, the event has been unsatisfactory. No one invites us any more.

I determine to go to our annual dinner with a singularity of purpose and brush aside all objections. The venue is a quaint little restaurant gained by a steep cobbled hill. The interior is dimly lit and 'ethnic'. 'I like to see what I am eating,' he grumbles.

What it lacks in comfort it more than compensates with

cheerful and careful artistry. There is plenty of pot-pourri, chintz and pine. We take our own wine. Out of the corner of my eye I see Peter creeping in, weighed down with a carrier bag containing as many cans of Scottish and Newcastle as a carrier can. I wonder how the corkage will be calculated here? La Patrona has only one menu which she chalks upon a board in a 'like-it-or-lump-it' gesture. We foregather with a glass of simply awful sherry, supplied by the management, which we drink for two reasons.

1. It has to be admitted it is horrendously cold in this damp old place. We have the place to ourselves and the stocking rate is not quite thick enough to generate heat.
2. It is free.

We soon get down to the serious business, assemble at tables and take up our implements. Here comes the first course. Petronella is a first-class cook and prides herself on 'doing everything'. Although praiseworthy, this does result in long waits between courses, during which time, if you are not very careful, you can find yourself slipping under the table. The food is beautiful.

'Pretentious rubbish. This isn't courgettes, is it? I don't believe it. I have had enough bloody courgettes in the summer to last at least one winter, if not several. . . .'

Pete is in good form though, jokes coming thick and fast; by the time we reach the pudding, they are purplish, and by coffee, which he declines, they are bright blue. No one seems to mind. The company is decidedly noisy by this stage. Strange, isn't it?

'Is that you, Veronica?'

'Er, yes.' The instantly recognisable tones of our neighbour up the hill can only mean one thing: trouble. I wait patiently.

'There have been some unsavoury characters on my land. They said you had given them permission to go after rabbits. Is this true?'

'Er – yes.'

For some years now, groups of youths have come up from Newcastle from time to time, accompanied by a ferret or two. We are happy that the pests are being controlled. The boys are happy to have a day in the open air and as they are often out of work, the price of a corpse or two comes in handy. Up till now, it has only been the rabbits who were not happy. It is true that some of the visitors present a slightly weird appearance, with their shaved heads and ear-rings, and it is true that one or two look as if a spot of soap and water wouldn't come amiss. But on the whole, they are polite and pleasant and, in any case, we see little of them. Of course, from time to time, there is always the odd 'cowboy'. The one who goes where he shouldn't, the one who brings a gun . . . but this happens rarely. They are told.

'Well, Veronica, I told them to get off my land – and they gave me a whole lot of abuse. I am surprised at you. . . .' On he grumbles, and it gradually dawns on me that *I* am responsible for his discomfiture. No doubt I have summoned these indolent layabouts from the city and set them to lay waste his land. I leave him talking into thin air.

The youths keep coming. One lot arrives early on Saturday morning, parking their car outside the house. At nightfall it is still there. I am just brushing my teeth prior to retiring when overheard voices at the door indicate that there has been a little problem. One of the ferrets has cornered an unfortunate rabbit, deep down in the bowels of the earth, and neither is able to be reached. Rather than return to town ferretless, they decide to spend the night in their car and try again at dawn. They announce their success with relief at 9 am and depart.

'I phoned the wife last night,' he says in his deep Geordie tongue, 'and she said she'd heard *some* excuses in her time but. . . .'

Every mother knows the school Nativity play/carol service which the first schools stage each year. All children are involved. At this one, the youngest children sit or stand in silent tableau at one side. Presumably they are not considered to be trusted, and my own experience of the age group involved leads me to agree with this policy.

Oh dear, that dressing gown looks – er, well – rather like a dressing gown, I suppose. The towel arranged on the head is a masterly stroke but I suspect might come uncoiled in the not-too-distant future. Another son stands holding his father's crook. I can tell from the expression on his face that he is becoming bored. His headgear slips to one side and teacher steps smartly forward to reposition it. Oh, is that how it was before?

Never mind, I can also divine that he is wondering what to do with that crook. No – you shouldn't have done that! 'Mary' looks round in some agitation as she has suddenly received a surprise sharp tap on the back of her head. I try to quell him with a look but his eyes refuse to meet mine or those of his teacher. This angelic little scene is in serious danger of becoming dismantled if we are not careful.

Meanwhile, centre stage the full thrust of the action is being undertaken by the Three Wise Kings, one of whom is still faintly recognisable, not to mention parts of his colourful costume. His hour is come at last. He is able to give full rein to his dramatic tendencies. He does deliver his lines with commendable clarity; his large blue eyes reach out to his audience from beneath his beautifully constructed cardboard crown. Ah, those eyes and that mouth – in which butter wouldn't dare to melt!

This child has the enviable facility of being able to disclaim knowledge of any crime for which there is a wealth of evidence piled against him, not to mention more than one reliable witness, with a look of complete innocence. It is so convincing that you begin to wonder if everyone else *is* plotting against him, or if we have all suffered the same mental aberration. He will go far. An actor? A lawyer? A politician?

Ah, we are clapping. It is all over. Mothers exchange

looks and comments about the performances of their off-spring and we file slowly out of the warm hall into the cold night.

The term is over. In the few days between this joyful occasion and the big event, this mother, in common I suspect with many others, begins to feel ill. The children are over-excited, edgy, tearful and demanding; there is still *so much to do*, and she has the overriding impression that she is totally alone. Somehow, these last few days, work outside has stepped up dramatically, even after dark. . . .

At last, it is Christmas Eve. It does not feel like Christmas at all, but then it never does these days. Nevertheless, I feel bound to spend some time heating up the holiday cottage as it has lain vacant for some weeks and people are due today. Brrr . . . yes – these damp old stone buildings soon get cold; it feels infinitely warmer outside than in. I light the fires upstairs, and down and back and forth I trek all day, keeping them topped up, this activity mingled with the traditional ones of mincepie making, present wrapping, decoration titivating, preparation of stuffings, etc. A feeling of panic tends to sweep through your whole being – a sort of asphyxia – and if I hear 'Jingle Bells' once more on the radio or see one more advert for a space ship implanter, which someone wants and is not getting, I'll scream. The whole thing seems like some vast psychiatric torture. . . .

No – there is one short breathing space: the ritualised trip to Uncle Gordon's farm, further into the hills, for the purpose of collecting the tree. The house is relatively quiet for about an hour. It would be too much to expect the interval to be any longer as we have Uncle Gordon's farm, house and general state of health to consider too. Nevertheless, I make yet another trip to the holiday cottage. It is late afternoon. They should be here soon. The fires are well established and heat is radiating through the house at last. Now for the final touches: the plate of freshly made mincepies by the fireside, the bottle of wine, the holly. As I return to the house, I see

213

the B.O.V. returning laden with children and tree. It's a big one this time, isn't it?

'No bigger than usual,' he says as he carries it round to the front door.

'Why are you sawing that piece off then?'

'Just to correct the tilt.'

What does it matter? Here is the old box of decorations, and at last our tree is finished to the best of our abilities and resources. There seem fewer decorations this year, or is the tree bigger? The end result is therefore a bit bare but once the lights are added, it seems to satisfy.

The children are now in bed. They are not asleep or even quiet but they have now been banished from the lower regions on pain of an empty stocking. They have their 'stockings' in place. I use the word loosely, each having chosen his own receptacle for Santa's bounty, varying in size from a massive plastic bag which previously contained a mattress to a more modest pillowcase. The younger children still believe in Santa; the older ones would like to. Therefore, they seem more than a little disturbed by the fact that Samson and Them blocked up their fireplace in summer. This situation requires some sensitive handling and complex explanations are put forward as to the gentleman's point of entry. They seem satisfied.

I feel totally exhausted. I have wrapped all the presents, running out of paper, the last ones being covered in flower-encrusted wallpaper. I don't suppose it matters, the stuff is just ripped off in a frenzy anyway. I have not completed all the preparations for the meal as I intended. I wrote out a list this morning of everything I had to do, a practice which has always worked well on busy days such as christenings. Today, the writing covered three pages and when I reached Job No. 63, I gave up writing. I have now given up everything, ground to a halt.

I have a friend (why do I have such efficient and artistic friends?) who not only has all her culinary preparations completed on Christmas Eve but also has her table beautifully laid, silver and crystal winking against the polished background of mahogany, candles, holly, crackers completing the picture. My dining room table is still covered with parcels, Sellotape and scrap paper.

A thought flits through my head that the holiday cottagers must have gone direct to source, passing 'go' on the way; they have been before and the keys are in the door. I close the dining room door with its usual resonant click. I close the kitchen door. I close the sitting room door behind me as I collapse into a chair beside the – er – fire.

'What's happened to the fire?'

'Well, it's not cold, is it?'

It is not. The weatherman on the television smiles and says that the mild weather will continue over Christmas. William Hill is quite confident of his 1000:1 on a White Christmas. I don't know about white Christmases but I wouldn't object to one of those clean frosty mornings with a sparkling day thereafter. That is what I would like for Christmas, but it's a bit late to ask now I suppose. The frontal systems and areas of high and low pressure, isobars and all that sort of thing are already in place, so to speak, ready for the Big Day – which I am not, but which I have decided not to think about for the moment.

'Yes, I *will* have a drink.'

'Have we got any?'

'Have we got any? This is Christmas, dear. Where is your Christmas spirit?'

'It's much like any other day to me.'

Huh, well, to all other members of this household, it ain't. Hello, there's the phone.

'What's that? You have decided not to come until Boxing Day? I see.'

I'll tell you something, I announce to no one in particular after I have replaced the receiver. Christmas spirit or no Christmas spirit, goodwill towards all men and all that . . . I am just leaving things exactly as they are in the cottage. What a time to tell me! Stale mincepies and the charred remains of a fire do not look so attractive, as I can see for myself, sitting here. A few sips of amber liquid from my glass and it's a case of:

'Wake up. Wake up, dear. Baby is crying and I am going to bed.'

'Er what? What about the presents?'

'Oh yes – I forgot!'

Forgot!

We stumble round, spreading good cheer equally (I hope) throughout the household, attend to Baby and finally fall into a deep if uncomfortable sleep, only to be wakened after what seems minutes but is probably a few hours, and this is the start of The Day.

I am tempted to retain complete unconsciousness beneath the bedclothes like their father, who is not acting. Unfortunately, a reflex borne of many years' experience propels me into automatic action the minute a child enters the bedroom, and I am a poor actress anyway. It is Sons Numbers Two and Three coming towards me at . . . let me see – 3.25 am.

'Go back to bed!' I groan. 'Try to get back to sleep!' Fat chance. I suppose that it matters little if they open their stockings (their 'foreign' presents are downstairs under the tree in piles to be opened later), as long as they wake no one else. Do you think they might even go back to sleep?

Anyway, they return to their rooms and my eyelids fall once more with relief. The next thing I know is that I am bombarded with, 'Look, Mummy, look!' and find the horrendously angular space toy I only wrapped hours before about six inches from the end of my nose. I look at the clock again: 5.55 am. Well, could be worse; I have experienced worse.

The level of noise round about indicates that I had better get up. Shrieking, fighting, punching, crying, together with loud sounds of tearing paper and rattling. Yes, be brave. If order is not established now, I'll lose control and the whole of Christmas Day will collapse. I pull on one of his old sweaters (I have long abandoned the search for a presentable dressing

gown to fill all requirements). How can he be oblivious to
it all? There he lies – a motionless lump in the bedclothes
(more than his share as usual) snoring quietly, an expression
of benign innocence on his face, the visible part that is. The
sight which meets the eyes in the boys' rooms bears some
resemblance to the aftermath of the Little Bighorn. Oh yes –
The Day has begun all right.

By the time Sleeping Beauty descends the stairs to start his
day, ours has been in full swing for hours. The 'stockings'
have all been opened, the wrapping papers gathered up and
dealt with. 'They' have been forcibly restrained at intervals
from embarking upon the piles in the hall, the necessary
agent for the opening ceremony having been absent. Actually
it is difficult to see the piles, let alone reach them, because
of the enormous tree. Never have they been so pleased to
greet their parent; he seems quite touched by their sudden
affection, poor soul. A mass dive moves past him through
into the hall.

'Mind the tree!'

It is all too much. Is it too early for a drink? Do you know,
he manages to be out of the door around his usual time,
having filled himself with his usual breakfast, manufactured
from nowhere. Luckily, no one else is interested in the meal.

Ah, the weather has changed – so much for that creep at
the Weather Centre. He sniffs the keen morning air appre-
ciatively. Then, he summons the dogs to heel – nice to have
someone doing as he is told – and off he goes round the
sparkling, frost-encrusted fields.

What he leaves behind the farmhouse door is another
story. There is no floor visible in the kitchen or hall –
just a sea of torn paper robins, holly and bells. Already,
signs of tiredness are beginning to appear. We are entering
that all-too-familiar anticlimax period, when this act of
unwrapping which has been eagerly awaited for months is
over. There is a touch of 'we-didn't-really-want-that-beauti-
fully-illustrated-educational-book-on-Roman-history; would-
much-prefer-to-have-had-that-super-radio-gun-as-advertised

on-TV-thank-you-very-much.' Then we have, 'Can you help me with this Lego fort?' and a staccato cry indicates that something is broken already. That book of puzzles seems to have been a minor triumph, thank goodness; someone is sitting quietly on his bed, pencil poised.

'No – don't do that!'

'Leave him alone!'

'Don't tear it!'

By the time I have cleared up the wrapping papers and tried to make a list of who has given what to whom, not to mention settled quarrels, repaired books, applied elastoplast, it is almost midday. Thank goodness I said I would do the meal in the evening. Before the boss returns, I manage to have done the vegetables and the stuffings and am feeling quite pleased with myself, if wilting very slightly.

Here he is, rosy of cheek, eyes sparkling. 'It's a lovely day. What's for lunch?'

I pretend I do not hear and he makes himself a cup of coffee, bemoaning the absence of papers. He then announces that he is going out to take another look at a cow about which he is dubious. I ask no questions, but it crosses my mind that I wouldn't mind going out for a bovine inspection myself. However, I have to concern myself with a slightly smaller farm creature.

Yes, the bird. I am sick of seeing it crouched in the fridge taking up an entire shelf and preventing easy closure of the door. Oh no, I don't believe it, I have run out of the magic medium without which we can no longer roast anything – *foil*! Short of suicide attempts, frothing at the mouth, hysteria, I cast back in my tired brain to something I once read about encasing the unfortunate in a paste manufactured from flour and water. After the appropriate cooking time, the paste is merely cracked open, leaving a succulent bird beneath, full of juices and flavour. It is worth a try. I have nothing to lose.

'Are you cooking Christmas dinner or doing a spot of wallpapering?' he asks on his way past to phone the vet. I ignore this, and neither do I indicate any interest in the welfare of those outside. This looks about the right consistency. I am almost enjoying myself as I smooth it over the breast with artistry.

'Oh, can I have a go?'

'Can I have some?'

It is inserted into the oven with a prayer and attention is turned elsewhere. Mercifully, Mother is bringing the pudding – not that anyone eats it in this house, with one exception. Now, there is a slight logistical problem: how to seat fifteen round a table which seems to baulk at ten?

'We've done it loads of times . . . at Christmases and things we used to have. . . .'

He is referring to the far-off distant past when there was another regime, another era; when it was always deep and crisp and even outside, no doubt. No doubt either that the table was set with nothing less than Edinburgh crystal and solid silver, sparkling upon white damask.

It is finally agreed to seat some of the younger members of the party at a smaller table to one side. It is a little congested in this corner but the arrangement meets with the approval of those concerned. The finished product may not bear comparison with the table of my friend or the one of yesteryear but it will do. The bone handles on my good silver plate are wobbly, due to their frequent trips round the dishwasher before I realised they should not. The glasses are not only not crystal but some are not even glass; the remainder gifted by means of the purchase of petrol from a local garage. Crackers we have, thanks to a kind cousin who sends them from afar every year without fail, and I have even attempted to decorate the table with holly and candles. It does not look too bad. Pity we have not quite enough chairs. I close the door quickly.

Hello, here he is again. 'What's that? Not a calving surely? Not on Christmas Day! I bet Alistair is thrilled to bits about that! Er – is the outcome a happy one?'

'Well, touch and go. I'll have to keep a close eye on them

over the next day or two.'

'I bet you will! Was it a boy or a girl?'

'A good bull calf. Enormous. That was the trouble.'

'You'd better call him Noel.'

'Eh?'

'Noel, dear. Christmas baby and all that.'

'Ah, yes. I am exhausted. I think I'll go and have a bath.'

'Yes, I should.'

Without further ado, he disappears, clutching one of his presents from Santa – the latest Dick Francis. He reappears approximately forty-eight minutes later, looking pink and refreshed, leaving a greenish-brown ring round the bath.

'Anything to do, Dear?'

'You can take over when they arrive and I collapse in a heap on the floor.'

In the event I do no such thing, of course. Here we are all congregated in the kitchen. Why don't they go somewhere else? I hate people watching me trying to extract lumps from the gravy or replace vegetables fallen on the floor in the serving dishes. I know it is warmer here than anywhere else in the house, central heating or not. It must be mentioned that the man of the house is busy dashing (well, perhaps 'dashing' is a bit strong) round filling glasses, talking and listening, watching the children and correcting any deviation from acceptable behaviour.

Oh no – several guests are now leaning against the Aga – whilst the cook is frantically switching stuff from oven to oven. Now is the hour of reckoning – the bird! Now my mind is muddled by sherry, I wonder if it was perhaps hedgehogs I was thinking about? I do hope no one is watching. The paste shroud is brownish, bordering on black.

'Why is it burnt, Mummy?'

To hell with hanging about. With one flourish, I raise the carving knife in the air and bring it down – crack – on to the blackened bird. Full marks for dramatic effect anyway. The creature inside the case is certainly cooked; it disintegrates totally under the knife and the paste shatters into a thousand pieces. I strain the juices of their indigestible flotsam and pour into gravy boat. Throughout all I retain a fixed smile on my face as if all his was meant to happen.

At last, we are ready. The bird, even if it does look a little down, is embellished thickly with parsley and surrounded by glistening sausages and bacon rolls. All accompaniments look OK.

'Ugh!'

'I don't want any of *that*!'

'Aren't there any beans/chips/ice cream?'

I don't know really why I bothered with the small table. Never mind, they seem quite happy to sit there, pull their crackers and don their paper hats, swapping jokes and novelties.

Whoops – I nearly forgot the candles.

'What are you doing? I can't see what I am eating.'

The meal proceeds with jollity. The wine supplied by my brother is rather superior to our usual stuff, and we do appreciate it.

However, at the end of the day, I ask myself is it really worth it? The mountains of dirty plates and glasses – all this work for a mere *meal*? It is simply too much to have Christmas dinner on Christmas Day – and this is the truth. Well, we battle on. . . .

Now, the guests have gone home, the children are all asleep, exhausted, at last, and he is sitting with his feet up beside the fire, with a glass of another present from Santa in his hand, watching the classic Western. I don't know why. Apart from the fact that he has in all probability seen it before, the footage is punctuated with triumphant shrieks of,

'Look: there's a Friesian', or

'That field hasn't been ploughed by hand!'

I smile as I drift off to sleep.